The

Year

of the

Poet X

May 2023

The Poetry Posse

inner child press, ltd.

The Poetry Posse 2023

Gail Weston Shazor

Shareef Abdur Rasheed

Teresa E. Gallion

hülya n. yılmaz

Kimberly Burnham

Tzemin Ition Tsai

Elizabeth Esguerra Castillo

Jackie Davis Allen

Joe Paire

Caroline 'Ceri' Nazareno

Ashok K. Bhargava

Alicja Maria Kuberska

Swapna Behera

Albert 'Infinite' Carrasco

Michelle Joan Barulich

Eliza Segiet

William S. Peters, Sr.

~ * ~

In order to maintain each poet's authentic voice, this volume has not undergone the scrutiny of editing. Please take time to indulge each contributor for their own creativity and aspirations to convey their uniqueness.

hülya n. yılmaz, Ph.D.
Director of Editing ~
Inner Child Press International

The Year of the Poet X
May 2023 Edition

The Poetry Posse

1ˢᵗ Edition : 2023

Publisher Information
1ˢᵗ Edition : Inner Child Press
intouch@innerchildpress.com
www.innerchildpress.com

Copyright © 2023 : The Poetry Posse

ISBN-13 : 978-1-952081-97-2 (inner child press, ltd.)

$ 12.99

WHAT WOULD LIFE BE WITHOUT A LITTLE POETRY?

Dedication

This Book is dedicated to

Humanity, Peace & Poetry

the Power of the Pen

can effectuate change!

&

The Poetry Posse

past, present & future,

our Patrons and Readers &

the Spirit of our Everlasting Muse

In the darkness of my life
I heard the music
I danced . . .
and the Light appeared
and I dance

Janet P. Caldwell

Table of Contents

The Poetry Posse

Table of Contents . . . *continued*

May's Featured Poets 115

Inner Child Press News 143

Other Anthological Works 181

Foreword

Children: Difference Makers

Louis Braille

From the Encyclopedia Britannica we learn that Louis Braille was born in Coupvray, near Paris, France on the 4th of January 1809. As a renown French educator, he would pass away, in Paris, two days after his 43rd birthday, on the 6th of January, 1852.

While in his father's harness shop, at the age of 3, he had an accident. A tool he was playing with slipped and plunged into his right eye. As a result, he became blind in both eyes. A condition called, sympathetic ophthalmia.

Louis Braille received a scholarship, and in 1919, attended the National Institute for Blind Children in Paris. Interested in a system of writing utilizing dots on cardboard, at the age of 15, he adapted one by Charles Barbier, making it his own, adapting it further to musical notation. He taught at that same school from 1826. It is thanks to him that many who were and are blind were finally able to read.

Despite being blind, he published a 3-volume Braille edition of a history book, popular at the time. Additionally, he became a well known musician, and as an excellent organist. It is interesting that a century after his death, his remains (except his hands which stayed in Coupvray, his birthplace) were moved to Paris where they were buried in the Pantheon, Paris. (He had been ill with tuberculosis in his last years.)

Jackie Davis Allen

Author ~ Artist

Preface

We, **Inner Child Press International, The Year of the Poet** and **The Poetry Posse** welcome you.

We are so excited as we are now offer unto you our fourth month of our **10th** year of monthly publication of this enterprise, **The Year of the Poet**.

For those of you who are not familiar with our story, back in 2013, a few of us poets got together with the simple intention of producing a book a month. That was our challenge. Since that time the enterprise has blossomed and brought forth a fruit that seems to keep on growing as evidenced as we enter 2023.

Our purpose is simple. Through our lyrical words and verse, we not only wish to share our poetic works, but we also have the poetic naiveté to believe that we can assist in the growth of consciousness of the things that have an effect our collective humanity. Therefore, we welcome your readership. For more about what we are attempting to accomplish, have a look at our Publishing Web Site . . . www.innerchildpress.com. If you would like to know a bit more about this particular endeavor please stop by for a visit at :
www.innerchildpress.com/the-year-of-the-poet

Over the years, Inner Child Press has been socially active to bring awareness and catalog through literature the things that have an impact upon our world and its inhabitants. We have solicited, produced, underwritten and published quite a few volumes to that end. For more insight you may wish to visit : www.innerchildpress.com/the-anthology-market. If you are a writer, poet, or activist, you would be advised to keep a eye out for upcoming volumes should you desire to participate. All readers are welcomed as well. Note, that there is a myriad of published volumes that are available as a FREE PDF download as well as available for purchase at affordable prices.

We at this time extend to you our well wishes for your own personal journey and hope that you consider including us as a travel companion.

Bless Up

Bill

William S. Peters, Sr.

Publisher
Inner Child Press International
www.innerchildpress.com

Children
Difference Makers
Louis Braille
May 2023

by Kimberly Burnham, Ph.D.

Louis Braille was only 12 when he learned of a communication system used by the French army, which laid the groundwork for his own system of reading and writing used by the blind. He completed his alphabet of raised dots by the time he was 15. It was first adapted by France's Royal Institute for Blind Youth until two years after his death at the age of 43. It has since spread throughout the world and is still in use today.

~ * ~

"Braille is knowledge, and knowledge is power."
~Louis Braille

"Access to communication in the widest sense is access to knowledge, and that is vitally important for us if we are not to go on being despised or patronized by condescending sighted people. We do not need pity, nor do we need to be reminded that we are vulnerable. We must be treated as equals — and communication is the way we can bring this about." ~Louis Braille

Poets . . .
sowing seeds in the
Conscious Garden of Life,
that those who have yet to come
may enjoy the Flowers.

Poets, Writers . . . know that we are the enchanting magicians that nourishes the seeds of dreams and thoughts . . . it is our words that entice the hearts and minds of others to believe there is something grand about the possibilities that life has to offer and our words tease it forth into action . . . for you are the Poet, the Writer to whom the Gift of Words has been entrusted . . .

~ wsp

poetry is . . .

Poetry succeeds where instruction fails.

~ wsp

Now Available

Inner Child Press International
&
The Year of the Poet
present

Poetry

the best of 2022

Poets of the World

innerchildpressanthologies@gmail.com

Gail Weston Shazor

This is a creative promise ~ my pen will speak to and for the world. Enamored with letters and respectful of their power, I have been writing for most of my life. A mother, daughter, sister and grandmother I give what I have been given, greatfilledly.

Author of . . .

"An Overstanding of an Imperfect Love"
&
Notes from the Blue Roof

Lies My Grandfathers Told Me

available at Inner Child Press.

www.facebook.com/gailwestonshazor
www.innerchildpress.com/gail-weston-shazor
navypoet1@gmail.com

Tip and Tap

Sometimes the clearest thing
Is that which is not seen
We feel our way through
Our tastes and memories
Collecting sounds by the crossroads
Hearing the good while
Discarding the painful
We can know the world
By using what we think is the least
Of understanding
That in most circumstances
Is the overstanding
Is it hot?
There are only clues in seeing
There are only clues in hearing
Ah but to feel is the truth
Fingertaps connect our hearts
To our universe
Fingertips show us the way

Thunder and Lightening

Sterling flashes against green
Where just a sliver of light
Finds its way into loam
The depression created
By thunder bounces
Against the sky erratically
And I reach for your hand
Winding my breath around
The forefinger and thumb
Because I want my heart held
We talk of sex
With the honesty of expectations
That occur naturally and with a
Spontaneity in a lifetime
Of familiarity
Time has no hold on this
Our kinetic friendship
Because I knew you
Long before I was meant
For you to find in places unlooked
It is here in the darkest moments
With your back against
The sturdy spine of trees
I can fit inside the palms
That rest against the bent hip
Of my softness, gentleness
The coaxing of calmness
Against the temperance of a quickening
And I am no longer alone
Within this lightening storm
I keep hidden those words
Said in haste but always

Measured against the moment
Of someone else's parting
Of our enclosed solitude
The pain of which has faded
In learning what is important about
My heart locked into the space
Between thumb and forefinger
And yours ever in my soul

Heart Wynd

Heart wynd crossroads
Tall grows the wall
Voice and mind says
Yet and
Knows no edges
Misunderstanding not
Kisses stolen
Skin to skin want
Light of dawn
SLEEPING
Dawn of light
Want skin to skin
Stolen kisses
Not misunderstanding
Edges no knows
And yet
Says mind and voice
And the wall grows tall
Crossroads wynd heart

Gail Weston Shazor

Alicja Maria Kuberska

Alicja Maria Kuberska – awarded Polish poetess, novelist, journalist, editor.

She is a member of the Polish Writers Associations in Warsaw, Poland and IWA Bogdani, Albania. She is also a member of directors' board of Soflay Literature Foundation, Our Poetry Archive (India) and Cultural Ambassador for Poland (Inner Child Press, USA)

Her poems have been published in numerous anthologies and magazines in : Poland, Czech Republic, Slovakia, Hungary,Ukraina, Belgium, Bulgaria, Albania, Spain, the UK, Italy, the USA, Canada, the UK, Argentina, Chile, Peru, Israel, Turkey, India, Uzbekistan, South Korea, Taiwan, China, Australia, South Africa, Zambia, Nigeria

She received two medals - the Nosside UNESCO Competition in Italy (2015) and European Academy of Science Arts and Letters in France (2017). Ahe also received a reward of international literary competition in Italy „ Tra le parole e 'elfinito" (2018). She was announced a poet of the 2017 year by Soflay Literature Foundation (2018).She also received : Bolesław Prus Prize Poland (2019), Culture Animator Poland (2019) and first prize Premio Internazionale di Poesia Poseidonia- Paestrum Italy (2019).

Louis Braille
Inconspicuous dots

In a world of darkness,
touch and hearing
lead through life.
Of bumps on the paper
letters hatch out
dance under fingers
and join into words.

The written world
opened wide its gates,
invited to the library paradise.
It led through the labyrinth
made of dots.

The silent books spoke.
They shared
reflections of great thinkers,
recited beautiful stanzas of poems
passed on knowledge,
they entertained and taught.

For the uninitiated,
they are only dots in rectangles.
Brilliant inventions amaze
with their simplicity

Rain

It rains,
and drops flow
through the fingers
like time
like memories
like the atoms of life.

Prayers
requests or entreaties won't help
- nothing can stop the downpour.

More drops fall.
Hours and days
run between fingers.
Past moments fade away
and people sink into the ground.

September in Kazimierz Dolny

Autumn added baroque splendor to the city.
It repainted the leaves in titian colors,
gave the clouds Rubensian shapes.

The sun gilded
the Renaissance tenement houses.
Glittering rays poured out
between the shingles of the old houses,
sprinkled the waves of the Vistula
with silver brocade.

Time settled down on the steps of the parish church
It listened to the slow rhythm of the streets
and memories of an old town well
about a faithful dog and two moons.

The minutes stopped.
The hours passed slowly.

The clock was ticking:
no need to rush
run ahead.
What for?
It's beautiful here.

Jackie
Davis
Allen

Jackie Davis Allen, otherwise known as Jacqueline D. Allen or Jackie Allen, grew up in the Cumberland Mountains of Appalachia. As the next eldest daughter of a coal miner father and a stay at home mother, she was the first in her family to attend and graduate from college. Her siblings, in their own right, are accomplished, though she is the only one, to date, that has discovered the gift of writing.

Graduating from Radford University, with a Bachelor's of Science degree in Early Education, she taught in both public and private schools. For over a decade she taught private art classes to children both in her home and at a local Art and Framing Shop where she also sold her original soft sculptured Victorian dolls and original christening gowns.

She resides in northern Virginia with her husband, taking much needed get-aways to their mountain home near the Blue Ridge Mountains, a place that evokes memories of days spent growing up in the Appalachian Mountains.

A lover of hats, she has worn many. Following marriage to her college sweetheart, and as wife, mother, grandmother, teacher, tutor, artist, writer, poet and crafter, she is a lover of art and antiques, surrounding herself, always, with books, seeking to learn more.

In 2015 she authored *Looking for Rainbows, Poetry, Prose and Art*, and in 2017, *Dark Side of the Moon*. Both books of mostly narrative poetry were published by Inner Child Press and were edited by hulya n. yilmaz in 2019, *No Illusions. Through the Looking Glass*, which was nominated to be considered for a Pulitzer Prize by the publisher and editor of Inner Child Press, ltd.

http://www.innerchildpress.com/jackie-davis-allen.php
jackiedavisallen.com

Gift of Discovery

What is this void of light
That raises its hands, like
A warning, a sign conveying,

Stop! Go no further! Yet, searching
For a way to see, to read
That which is not visible?

Beyond this point a wall, for some, stands
Impregnable, where something forbidden,
Incomprehensible, actually exists.

And, where on one side of that wall,
Images commonly accessible to most,
Are tragically denied to others.

A choice? Only the one found
In hopes desire, arising as from
heart and mind's desperation.

A method, found, discovered.
Then conveyed. Like a precious gift, given
As met from one's genius's effort and need.

It remains a gift to any
Who would exert the effort,
Available to one and all.

Those born with. Or without.

Put the Chicken and Dumplings On

Skeletal fingers tracing my face,
Voice dripping with love's care,
With unseeing eyes. I'm remembering, how
She embraced my childhood's wondering innocence.

With milky-white, translucent-skin,
Failing, thin, white strands
Falling upon her aged brow, her delicate
Fingers served as her eyes.

For eyes and sight that had dimmed,
Despite poverty's environment, and its distance,
She replaced her losses with a love
And care beyond my comprehension.

With little schooling, (obviously with no degrees),
Deprived of art, literature, poetry, travel,
Her days were filled with songs, prayers.
And the present-past: the joy of expectant visitors.

"The geese are a'coming, she'd say.
Put the chicken and dumplings on."
And without plans, correspondence, or phone,
Somehow she knew when my family would arrive.

I called her "Grandma". However could that be?
Who or where was the Grandpa?
More than a half century would pass before
I discovered she was my grandfather's step-mother.

The Dream

Twisted, gnarled branches
Silhouetted against the darkening sky.
Blackbirds flocking, squawking
Fleeing the sorrowful
Wind swept landscape
Of a dream's sigh.
Torrential rains
Striking, frightening, wounding.
Ravens hiding
Cawing, cawing, crying
Over the anticipated desire
For life's symphony.
Dayspring, summer flowers,
Sprouting, emerging;
Bluebirds chirping, singing
Returning, renewing
Nature, and desiring
Something more.
Hot, bright scalding light,
Stinging, burning notes
Composing, orchestrating
A song, a chorus
Of a future awakening
To possibilities.
Twisted, gnarled branches.
Torrential rains, dayspring, summer flowers.
Hot bright scalding light.
Tireless efforts revealing
Childhood's dream, now in sight

The original above was penned Feb.2011. It was published in 2019, in my book, No Illusions, Through the Looking Glass (Inner Child Press, Ltd.).

Tzemin
Ition
Tsai

Dr. Tzemin Ition Tsai comes from the Republic of China(Taiwan). In addition to being a professor of literature at a university, he is more committed to writing poems, novels, and proses. He is also an editor of "Reading, Writing and Teaching" academic text, an International editor of "Contemporary dialogues" literary periodical in Macedonia, and Vice-Chairman of the International Jury of the SAHITTO INTERNATIONAL AWARD in Bangladesh, and a columnist for "Chinese Language Monthly" in Taiwan.

In a wide range of literary creations, he is particularly fond of interesting stories or novels, and writing articles or poems about the feelings of nature and human beings. He has won many national literary awards. His literary works have been anthologized and published in books, journals, and newspapers in more than 55 countries and have been translated into more than 24 languages.

Accompany Me To Greet The Lonely Return Boat

This bay
I watched for a cycle of sixty years
Always calm, except when the ship enters port
Who is meddlesome and lead into the lovesickness?
Nowadays, more and more cars and horses go back and
forth
The childhood scene no longer seen
Indulge me, a wanderer in deep autumn, to rest in the shade
Feel different today
Especially
In front of my eyes, like a calm mirror in colorful clothes

Remember?
When you were a little girl
We run on the beach together
You were always restless, going back and forth
At that time
Mother is always waiting at home

Now
The returning clouds are sparse, the mountains and rivers
look like they used to
No mother waiting at home
That layer of mist that couldn't be thinner
But it will really make people unable to get up
Oops
Really make me unable to get up

Always curious
Except for that rainbow
Except for the small boat under the arch bridge
Except for this sea with no any tiny bit of waves
what else did you see?

Peek Into The Sky

The sound of the waves over the beach rising and falling
Sunny rain why didn't you fall generously
The pine trees are so tall, and the slanting shadows rotate
with the sun
The top of the mountain in the distance, white clouds like
snow
No dust at all
The tripod on the shoulder
Not an easy burden
imitate the overlapping rocks
Sojourn in this Wonderful Terrace
Through the lens, guide my greedy eyesight
Looking at the clouds and mountains poorly, nature will
also sprinkle beautiful articles
Lure me to pick it all up
Before I can't afford it

Reverse my camera
Let everything in the mirror be reflected up side down
A flock of swallows flies low, the intent to peep into the
sky is like an immortal's whispering
The sky is connected into one piece, all eaten into my lens
The mountain's broken clouds are green, and the water
flows on both sides
I have no good words
Pair with this amazing view
The scenery is so chaotic, I wander around and admire it
Forget the handover of the old man who lived on the cliff
Don't urge, don't urge
I'll surely be back when the wind blows again

The Grass Has Just Turned Green, The Herd Of Deer Competing For Color

The tent was left ruthlessly, and the clouds drifted away
The car passed through the valley of the mountaineering,
and turned around several times
Only then do I feel suddenly enlightened like the zenith
In the early spring of the prairie, the green is well-
proportioned, why blue dark and ignorant?
Who is snatching the colors under the blue sky?
Whose herdsmen are fighting to step on the grassy plain?
The sun is quiet and the wind is gorgeous
The green trees weigh down, the eagle hovering overhead
Floating among palm hills and mountains

The mountain, towering and steep, surrounds and does not
return
Orchid Island looks east to the mist, located behind the
Pacific Ocean
People in the world pursue prosperity and wealth and grow
old
How to know the elk's leisurely among the grass?
The wind blowing from the sea is warm
Can't let go of the smoke that can't fade away, coil lying on
the bed and feeling uneasy
Even singing poems to praise the herd of deer
Plum, you old bones, so what you still obsessed with the
officialdom games?

Even from today onwards, you can't walk like a deer and
read like an ant
Walking on the prairie with joyful singing
Absolutely unnecessary
The ego is trapped in a cage and barely speaks
Ask for the herd of sika deer overlooking the distance
Teach me how to be free

Shareef
Abdur
Rasheed

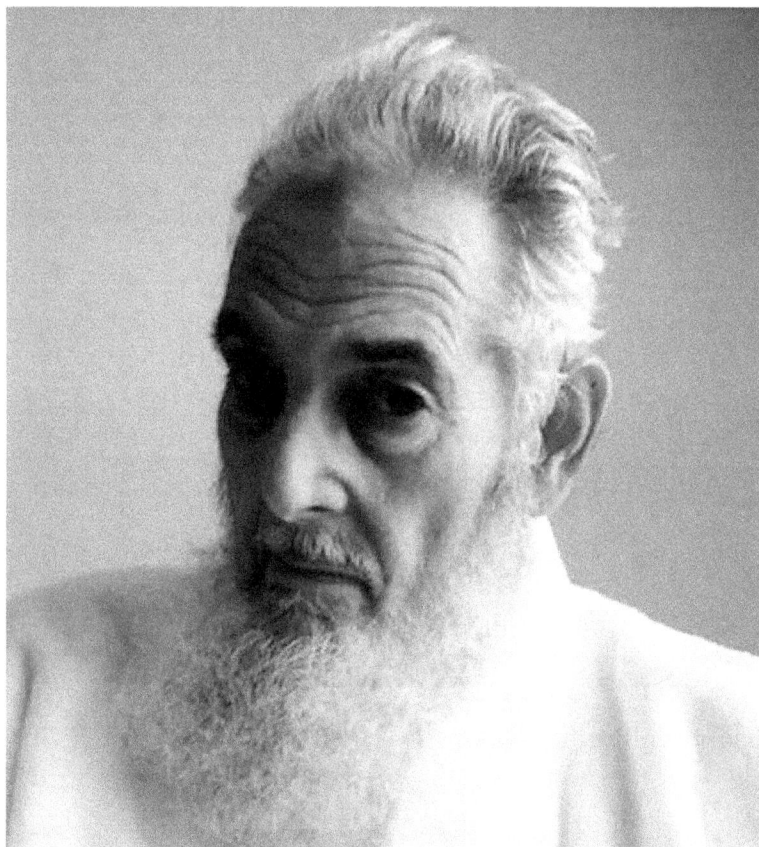

Shareef Abdur-Rasheed, AKA Zakir Flo was born and raised in Brooklyn, New York. His education includes Brooklyn College, Suffolk County Community College and Makkah, Saudi Arabia. He is a Veteran of the Viet Nam era, where in 1969 he reverted to his now reverently embraced Islamic Faith. He is very active in the Islamic community and beyond with his teachings, activism and his humanity.

Shareef's spiritual expression comes through the persona of "Zakir Flo" . Zakir is Arabic for "To remind". Never silent, Shareef Abdur-Rasheed is always dropping science, love, consciousness and signs of the time in rhyme.

Shareef is the Patriarch of the Abdur-Rasheed Family with 9 Children (6 Sons and 3 Daughters) and 41 Grandchildren (24 Boys and 17 Girls).

For more information about Shareef, visit his personal FaceBook Page at :

https://www.facebook.com/shareef.abdurrasheed1
https://zakirflo.wordpress.com

Braille

Born January 04, 1809
Coupvray, France
Death January 06 1852
Paris, France
Louis Braille
lost sight after
accident, infection
in spite excelled
as student
very young started
develop method
named after him
raised alphabet
letters allowed
blind students
to feel and identify
words and read
louis was genius
until now braille
is the most used
successful tool
worldwide
for the blind to be
able to read

Reflecting..,

on dem who reflect
bigups, respect
word sculptors
creative souls cut from
carefully woven rolls,
of fabric rare
manifested in sublime
rhyme, rhythm, prose
like Rakim i say
"let the rhythm hit em "
profound skill dem who
paint with words at will
who have profound
love beyond the pale
outside the box
what resides inside prevails
dem special folk provoke
introspective jubilees
such is the souls that delve
far below where others dare
not go
in places deep seeded
concepts grow out of
questions
demand answers
to mysteries that life hold
poets possess demanding souls
thirst and hunger to know

life be precious

magnificent, miracle grateful, grateful
never, i pray I will ever take for granted
this priceless beyond words gift of love, mercy,
kindness from above upon the highest from he
who is thee almighty
who in time of need or plenty says " call on me "
call on me i am closer to thee then your jugular
surely this gift is taken light, look at the horrific
accounts put out day and night
life blotted out like a bright light
world of might makes right
but no one has the right to terminate precious life
so much beauty to behold in abundance
all around us look up, look down, take a look around
this earth of ours has been blessed even with this mess
man has made of land and seascape
much remains to drink in contemplate how great
then give thanks to him only
as it is only he who can create
and look how he creates, look at what he makes
valleys, streams ,lakes, mountains, mighty, majestic
variety of living things to respect, love
birds flying above or on perch high above earth
a beautiful bouquet of hue
as in variety of color all around
from sky to light, look
profoundly...You...Me
audibly giving praise to thee
that's what all living things do regularly except
human beings that walk, talk, look like you and me
to the contrary mankind has intentionally, vocally,

locally, internationally
country to country say,
" it's me, me ,me "
not a surprise just look at history
as though he has created himself when in reality
he couldn't create anything, not even the smallest
microscopic organism
with naked eye one could not see
but one thing man can and will create is " Schism "
perpetually the schism of the ism
life is precious, protect, respect yours and your
brother and sister fellow human's life and limb
that will please him thee creator of precious life
peace/love/blessings

Shareef Abdur Rasheed

Kimberly Burnham

Kimberly Burnham

A brain health expert with a PhD in Integrative Medicine, Kimberly Burnham has lived in tropical Colombia; in Belgium during the Vietnam War; in Japan teaching businessmen English; in diverse international Toronto, Canada; and several places in the US. Now, she's in Spokane, WA with her wife, Elizabeth, two sets of twins (age 11 & 14) and three dogs. Her recent book, *Awakenings: Peace Dictionary, Language and the Mind, a Daily Brain Health Program* includes the word for peace in hundreds of languages. Her poetry weaves through 80+ volumes of *The Year of the Poet*, *Inspired by Gandhi*, *Women Building the World*, and *A Woman's Place in the Dictionary*. She is currently working on several ekphrastic writing projects. One is a novel, *Art Thief Cracks Healing Code for Parkinson's Disease* and the other is non-fiction, *Using Ekphrastic Fiction Writing and Poetry to Create Interest and Promote Artists, Writers, and Poets.*

http://www.NerveWhisperer.Solutions

https://healthy-brain.medium.com/bears-at-the-window-of-climate-change-d1fb403eeaf3

Braille

One man

Louis Braille changed the world

giving access to millions

a form of communication

power through knowledge

so that more may access their own creativity

and change the world for good

Blinded

We are blinded by light
by love and snow
by arrogance and greed

We see what we want to see
what we expect to see all the time
reality is a figment of our imagination
blinded by our own expectations

Easily blindsided
as if events, people and ideas can come
out of nowhere
not there then suddenly there

look really look
listen truly listen
feel genuinely feel
reality and see the good in the universe

Peacock Peace

Peace discovered
between the pages
of a book
a Wolof - English Dictionary

Peace "jaama" in Gambia
found between
"jaam" slave and "jaamba" for marijuana
"jaambaat" to complain

As if peace can be found
in freedom from slavery
drugs and expressing one's views
in the English found between
payment "pey"
and peacock "jambajoob"

As if money can buy peace
or perhaps sharing
the equitable division of money
respect and appreciation
of natural beauty
brings peace
at a public park open to all
contemplating light
feathers fanned out in courtship

Elizabeth E. Castillo

Elizabeth Esguerra Castillo is a multi-awarded and an Internationally-Published Contemporary Author/Poet and a Professional Writer / Creative Writer / Feature Writer / Journalist / Travel Writer from the Philippines. She has 2 published books, "Seasons of Emotions" (UK) and "Inner Reflections of the Muse", (USA). Elizabeth is also a co-author to more than 60 international anthologies in the USA, Canada, UK, Romania, India. She is a Contributing Editor of Inner Child Magazine, USA and an Advisory Board Member of Reflection Magazine, an international literary magazine. She is a member of the American Authors Association (AAA) and PEN International.

Web links:

Facebook Fan Page

https://free.facebook.com/ElizabethEsguerraCastillo

Google Plus

https://plus.google.com/u/0/+ElizabethCastillo

Blind Power

Having sight without vision is useless

The blind can be more powerful than anyone else

For what is the essence of having perfect eyes,

When we do not have the heart for humanity?

Braille, an inspiring figure,

Gave meaning to why kindness is

a language that the deaf can hear

And that the blind can see so clear.

Cleansing Rains

Dewey teardrops from heaven above falling
As I reminisce the life before I've been in
Brings me back memories of yesteryears
Of laughters still echoing and overflowing tears.
My heart skips a beat tuning in with your rhythmic sound
Splattering into bits as you melodiously hit the ground
No, it doesn't mean its pain I always think of
when you're here
But also of cleansing my soul of evil demons
I wish to disappear.
A rainbow may soon manifest itself
from the distant horizon
Coloring my world with magical hues giving me inspiration
After you have dared exit from
your magnanimous performance
Giving the stage now to King Sun
as another beautiful day is at a glance!

The Boy by the Waterfalls

I see you in one of my greatest dreamscapes,
Sitting on a huge rock facing the majestic waterfalls
As I emerge out of nowhere in a place called the Ruins,
Where an ancient, mystic castle used to stand tall
A witness to a great kingdom's sweet downfall.
A river runs through the debris of
this enchanting sanctuary,
Flowing from under a magical bridge
where I am about to cross
And there came to view, a vivid and
glimmering sight of you,
But I failed to see how you could have looked
For your back was facing me while
you immersed in soulful serenity.
I missed to behold how your eyes could have stared
beautifully at me
Or if you are lonely and needs someone to be just there to
listen,
As tears flow down your cheeks looking for answers in
beautiful solitude.
I was about to step on the rock you are sitting on to tap
your back and say "Hi!"
But then you vanished into thin air and what was left was
white smoke,
And the empty space you left-
the same spot I sat on and delved into my own
contemplation
Then a realization came upon me that you wanted me to
carefully view the waterfalls you have laid your eyes on.
The waterfalls signifying the ebb and flow of life,
Things happen every now and then, constant changes
inevitably take place

Every split second and in the mere blink of an eye,
But life continuously flows come what may
What matters is how we enjoy our journey,
And do not have regrets for what could have been, what
might have been
But simply cherish how things used to be.

Joe
Paire

Joe Paire

Joseph L Paire' aka Joe DaVerbal Minddancer . . . is a quiet man, born in a time where civil liberties were a walk on thin ice. He's been a victim of his own shyness often sidelined in his own quest for love. He became the observer, charting life's path. Taking note of the why, people do what they do. His writings oft times strike a cord with the dormant strings of the reader. His pen the rosined bow drawn across the mind. He comes full-frontal or in the subtlest way, always expressing in a way that stimulate the senses.

www.facebook.com/joe.minddancer

Just A Few Bumps

Some take for granted the joy of reading language
Ancient cave drawings, Egyptian hieroglyphics'
And to be more specific, it's the written word

The written, can't always be read.
A lack of education, could play apart
But deeper than a teacher, not seeing is hard

Louis Braille was only 12
when he delved into a communication system
Once used by the French army

(God bless his heart)
He created a system, an alphabet of raised dots
A method of reading and writing used by the blind. He
completed his alphabet, around age 15 in time
Until two years after his death at the age of 43.
It has since spread throughout the world
and is still apart of current history.

Louis Braille, blind at 3
It's amazing what days mean to heightened senses
What's more amazing is a child could invent this.
It was first adapted by
France's Royal Institute for Blind Youth
I call it proof, or at least a poem about
Inspired youth.

Where Do We Go?

Been there, done that, and history repeats itself
I wouldn't be lying if I saw a movie 100 times
And we humans tend to please ourselves
Where do we go, when do we go
for something different to relive ourselves?
Do we relive past lives, and relive past lies
in the back of a "Winnebago"

Or to coin a phrase "Glory Days"
Depending on one's history!
That could mean some gory days
Still not erased from your memories

Where do we go for a beer,
when beer's no longer here?
Depending on what state you're in
It may be illegal there

And what about a good book
I mean one without propaganda
Or propaganda-less
Paperback or hardcopy
Preferably not written by a propagandist
Or some lying, cheating,
double dealing, sell you water televangelist
Can you handle the change,
of the politically deranged?
Or travel to the moon and beyond,
just because this planet is drained
Where do we go, to rest our souls?
When we arrest the souls of the freedom.

Knock, Knock!

Bang, bang! Who's there?
I was scared to even ask, who's there
Private property, I thought he was robbing me
The gun laws says pop 'em see,
and ask questions later
I'm guaranteed to walk away free
Due to laws from my legislator

I'm a prejudiced hater, with a registered gun
Licensed to kill, from a political bill
The right to conceal, no matter how I feel
I could hop on the bus, and do as I will

Second amendment rights
For those who don't it right
For those who don't get it, right!
A change for the insane, who creep around at night
Opportunistic people,
who're just looking for a fight

Instead of stopping people with issues
we have parents in constant candlelit vigils
Mixed messages and dog whistles
antiquated laws on the books and still applicable
being implemented in modern times
I find that despicable, I find that I'm sick of you
sacrifice the many, just to please the few
knock, knock, bang, bang
another family in a row of pews

hülya
n.
yılmaz

hülya n. yılmaz

Professor Emerita, hülya n. yılmaz is a published author, literary translator, and Co-Chair and Director of Editing Services at Inner Child Press International. Her poetic work appeared in numerous anthologies of global endeavors and was presented at various literary events in the U.S. and abroad. In 2018, WIN honored yılmaz with an award of excellence. Since 2017, her two poems remain permanently installed in *Telepoem Booth* – a U.S.-wide poetic art exhibition. hülya finds it vital for everyone to seek a deeper sense of self, and writes creatively to attain a comprehensive awareness for and development of our humanity.

hülya n. yılmaz, a traveler on the journey called "life" . . .

Writing Web Site
https://hulyanyilmaz.com/

Editing Web Site
https://hulyasfreelancing.com

taking them for granted . . .

our eyes, that is;
in fact, do we not take
our entire body and its precious parts
for granted throughout our lives?

each of us laments about some ones and
some things as our natural inclination;
on some days, perhaps, just perhaps,
we realize that we had it good all along

imagine: you cannot take in your loved ones'
physical presence eye-fully because
you are deprived of your eye-sight,
or you look up at what others tell you
is a gorgeous sky after the rain,
up above, a multi-color bow and all . . .

taking them for granted . . .
our eyes, that is

At the Young Age of 12 . . .

Louis Braille made the acquaintance of the French army.
Or better yet, the teenager discovered its distinct system
of communiqué. Consequently, the 12-year-old's own
reading and writing technique surfaced . . . for the blind.

1824 was the year of this invention of raised dot codes.
The Royal Institute for Blind Youth of France adapted
Braille's tactile writing system first.

The year of 2023 has been at our doorsteps
for several months now.
The French educator's legacy lives on.

dirty eyes

Hazel mixed with green

my eyes were once called dirty

my hair? . . . do not ask!

Teresa E. Gallion

Teresa E. Gallion was born in Shreveport, Louisiana and moved to Illinois at the age of 15. She completed her undergraduate training at the University of Illinois Chicago and received her master's degree in Psychology from Bowling Green State University in Ohio. She retired from New Mexico state government in 2012.

She moved to New Mexico in 1987. While writing sporadically for many years, in 1998 she started reading her work in the local Albuquerque poetry community. She has been a featured reader at local coffee houses, bookstores, art galleries, museums, libraries, Outpost Performance Space, the Route 66 Festival in 2001 and the State of Oklahoma's Poetry Festival in Cheyenne, Oklahoma in 2004. She occasionally hosts an open mic.

Teresa's work is published in numerous Journals and anthologies. She has two CDs: *On the Wings of the Wind* and *Poems from Chasing Light*. She has published three books: *Walking Sacred Ground, Contemplation in the High Desert* and *Chasing Light*.

Chasing Light was a finalist in the 2013 New Mexico/Arizona Book Awards.

The surreal high desert landscape and her personal spiritual journey influence the writing of this Albuquerque poet. When she is not writing, she is committed to hiking the enchanted landscapes of New Mexico. You may preview her work at

http://bit.ly/1aIVPNq or *http://bit.ly/13IMLGh*

Gift to Read

You dear Louis Braille
were rejected for the brilliance
of the language of braille
to support the blind.

You never gave up
and your mark of excellence
blooming at the age of 15
became your legacy
after your demise.

The language of braille you developed
is used throughout the world today.
To assist and give the blind
the wonderful opportunity to read.

Floating in the Garden

In my secret garden,
all things grow with joy.
Gratitude rides in the wind
and I float in the ecstasy
of this garden of love.

No judgment nor pain resides here.
Only the unfolding Spirit
may soar among the trees.
I hug every tree I can,
whisper love notes to the bark
and I hear the whole forest
engaged in a song of joy.

I cannot contain the feeling
of gratitude that overwhelms me.
I shapeshift back to elf
and float through the forest
on my unicorn.

Intensity

I go to the top of the mountain
to look for love.
Love is following me.
I scream to the edge of my lungs.
Love where are you?

Love sends a curling wave on the wind
that wraps me in the luxury of bliss.
I release my thoughts.
I surrender to love's blanket
and my knees buckle and I bow.

Water pouring from my eyes
floods the mountainside.
I cannot speak.
I just soak in the moment more intense
than anything I have ever felt.

Ashok K. Bhargava

ASHOK BHARGAVA is a poet, writer, inspirational speaker and a literary consultant. He has attended poetry conferences in Italy, Turkey, India and Philippines. His latest book "Riding the Tide" about his battle with cancer has been translated and published in Arabic, Hindi, Telugu and Bengali languages. He is a contributing writer to several anthologies worldwide including World Poetry Almanac 2014. He has been published in numerous print and online magazines.

Ashok has won many accolades including Poet Ambassador to Japan, Kalidasa International award, World Poetry Lifetime Achievement award, Writers Beyond Borders Peace award and Tapsilog Leadership award for his community involvement. He is founder of Writers International Network Canada Society to discover, nourish, recognize and celebrate writers, poets and artists and to assist them to network with the community at large. He is the author of eight books of poetry and one anthology. He is Artist-in-Residence at Moberly Arts & Cultural Centre and also co-edits the literary section of The Link Newspaper.

Reading Without Seeing
Dedicated to Louis Braille

Your day was dark
As the night
In your eyes
There was no light

You never gave up
Your will to fight
And learnt to read
Without eyesight

You captured words
On your finger tips
You saw the expressions
Without seeing the lips

You inscribed your name
On the face of stone
Your legacy lives
Long after you are gone

Deep in your soul
You carried more light
Than all of us combined
And made our path clear and bright

Holy Immersion

Today is a colorful day,
blossoms bend like an arch
in the perfumed fresh wind.

Silky sun-rays are warm,
the birds fly around
with melodies of delight.

I step into crystal clear water
that has absorbed
ashes and bones of my ancestors.

It makes me realize
that I will reap eternity here
when it will absorb my ashes too.

I see distant things
as if they were close and
take a distanced view of close things.

Truth must be seen as
what it is,
not what I want it to be.

*This poem is inspired by the Hindus belief of submerging
deceased person's ashes in the Ganges river to free the
soul from the cycle of reincarnation.*

Alone but not Lonely

I grab my phone
Take a selfie
Edit and enhance
Post it on Facebook
For others
To see and like it.

Then wait for people
To comment on how happy
I am with my loneliness.

Sometimes I respond
With emoticons.

That starts a process of following
Other accounts
Other lonely people.

The problem with it is
There are too many likes
That adhere to me
like breathing adhere to life.

Caroline
'Ceri Naz'
Nazareno
Gabis

Caroline 'Ceri' Nazareno-Gabis

Caroline 'Ceri Naz' Nazareno-Gabis, author of Velvet Passions of Calibrated Quarks, World Poetry Canada International Director to Philippines is a multi-awarded poet, editor, journalist, educator, peace and women's advocate. She believes that learning other's language and culture is a doorway to wisdom.

Among her poetic belts include **Gabrielle Galloni Memorial Panorama International Youth Award 2022**, Panorama Youth Literary Awards 2020, 7th Prize Winner in the 19th, 20th and 21st Italian Award of Literary Festival; Writers International Network-Canada ''Amazing Poet 2015'', The Frang Bardhi Literary Prize 2014 (Albania), Poet Journalist Award 2014 (Tuzla, Istanbul, Turkey) and World Poetry Empowered Poet 2013 (Vancouver, Canada). She's a featured member of Association of Women's Rights and Development (AWID), The Poetry Posse, Galaktika Poetike, Asia Pacific Writers and Translators (APWT), Axlepino and Anacbanua. Her poetry and children's stories have been featured in different anthologies and magazines worldwide.

Links to her works:

http://panitikan.ph/2018/03/30/caroline-nazareno-gabis/

https://apwriters.org/author/ceri_naz/

http://www.aveviajera.org/nacionesunidasdelasletras/id1181.html

The Language of the Eyes
For Braille

You designed a delicate window
For sweet, sympathetic souls,
Like musical dots align
In the ribs of conversations,
Between me, you, and the universe.
In your hands dwell the spoken transits
Of the unknown and the unpredictable
Internal frame.
World outside ourselves
Reminding the blows of appreciative reflection--
''You are everything''
Amidst the frequency of polarities
In circumstances,
Life is happening and we create life
From the entangled glances
In our quantum of emotions.
Choose your canvas from the wide spectrum
Reality changes in the eyes of many,
You can pour the truth
From your heart,
You can sieve empty judgments
From the eyes of love.

Flowers for the Children

In the middle of the street, I can see
Small budding flowers on my feet
Standing still on a sunny day
Its beauty is a sign of relief.

Its petals are dry, the scent is fading
Whether its stems are already bending
It stays to be the one--remains the same
Tiny as I can hold, bigger as I can claim!

As days go by, the little flower seems to be old
Wrinkled petals, leaves no more
I learn this tiny but huge
No one can get, the inner beauty is gold

Many might say, life offers that and this
We have petals of pain, sometimes at ease
I am like a little flower.
I am the one, a gift of wonder.

the roundtable of peace

each and the many
have this heart to share
tongues, figures, and colors
are blessings of life to wear
if dark stands to light the table
all embrace the torch of love
one by one
hand in hand
side by side
heart to heart
empowering the seals
of peace
inspiring the lips
of compassion
on the humble seat of humanity.

Swapna Behera

Swapna Behera is a trilingual poet, translator, environmentalist, editor from India and author of seven books of different genres including one on children's literature on Environment. She is the recipient of International UGADI AWARD 2019, honoured from Gujurat Sahitya Akademi 2022, 2021 International Poesis Award of Honor as Jury, Pentasi B World Fellow Poet, Honoured Poet of India from Seychelles Government and International awards from Algeria, Morocco, Kajhakhstan, modern Arabic Literary Renaissance of Egypt, International Arts Council Argentina etc. Her stories, poems, articles are published in many International and National magazines and ezines. Her poem A NIGHT IN THE REFUGEE CAMP is translated into 67 languages. She has received over 60 National and International Awards. At present she is the Cultural Ambassador for India and South Asia of Inner Child and the life member of Odisha Environmental Society

Email
swapna.behera@gmail.com

Web Site
http://swapnabehera.in/

When dots transmit alphabets ……..

when dots become alphabets
they talk back
here came
a tactile writing system
for people who are visually impaired
equality is the slogan
even without sight there is vision
Louis Braille
a French educator invented braille
at the age of three his right eye was wounded
 by a cobbler's tool while playing
left eye became inflamed
he became blind
yet
he was a crisis manager
and devised
an ultimate source of learning by feeling
his legacy is
tactile six dots arranged in the rectangle to read and write
at the age of sixteen he invented this system
move on the fingers over a series of dots
if you touch the words
they will touch you back
the dots will transmit alphabets …..

Compact capsules

1.   be a vicious cyclone
to swallow whatever cometh
a droplet is also an ocean

2.   fire is within
Should one beg fire from the Sun?

3.   Aroma of light
May be melting self silently

4.   ask the life
the magnitude of love
death will reply

5.   peace is the butterfly
On the mast of a submarine
the cocoon is on the shore

6   the night a crusty seducer
but always exhales agile dawn

7.   I beg apology
I broke the traffic rules of your silent zone
You became a word

8.   Can blood be singular?
Can love be singular?
Can water be singular?
Can pain be singular?
Tears of one is tears of all

9. soil is pure
You threw polythene and made it impure
Jungle is pure
You touched it and made it ashes

10. beyond the planet
always a new galaxy
a new sonnet

autobiography of a prostitute

I dance; I sing
I seduce; I reuse
I recycle; I reduce
I carry your ego
I dehydrate; I tolerate
I uproot; I implant
I segregate
I assimilate
I bargain
I die to live
I live to die
I merge all religions
I am secular
I take my body
I smile to hide
I smoke to provoke
I drink your lusts
I pretend to love
I respect
I have to say "I love you"
I am a currency and a bank
I wash my liquid sins every moment
To be a solid statue for tomorrow
You say I am proactive
I say you are so handsome
You say I am a black spot in the civil society
I say I am just a stake holder of my lost chastity
I am a living poetry
Just learning each day, the foreplay
I feed my baby
buy insulin for my mother-in-law
acupressure my paralytic husband

I have my own ethics
I listen more
my customers
speak a lot of their tears and fears
I listen silently
they need a listener
And I need money…
I am a sex worker
my body is on the traffic square
waiting for a new night
my soul is with my family
waiting for a new dawn
I am in between
Waiting for a bright day ………….

Albert 'Infinite' Carrasco

Albert "Infinite The Poet" Carrasco is an urban poet, mentor and public speaker.

Albert believes his experience of growing up in poverty, dealing with drugs and witnessing murder over and over were lessons learnt, in order to gain knowledge to teach. Albert's harsh reality and honesty is a powerfully packed punch delivered through rhyme. Infinite grew up in the east part of the Bronx and still resides there, so he knows many young men will follow the same dark path he followed looking for change. The life of crime should never be an option to being poor but it is, very often.

Infinite poetry @lulu.com

Alcarrasco2 on YouTube

Infinite the poet on reverbnation

Infinite Poetry

http://www.lulu.com/us/en/shop/al-infinite-carrasco/infinite-poetry/paperback/product-21040240.html

Louis Braille

i was born on January 4, 1809, in Coupvray, France.
I wanted to see the world but just at three years old I began
to lose that chance. with opened eyes all i see is darkness due
to an accident and uveitis. Nevertheless, I became a musician
and excelled as an organist. In 1819 I was granted a
scholarship to attend the National Institute for Blind
Children, while I was there I picked up a system of writing,
exhibited by Charles Barbier. In 1826 I started to teach
children similar to me, the partially blind and those that
couldn't see. I knew i was bright and wanted to share my
light, so I invented another method for the blind to read and
write. that was by embossing 63 characters on paper that
could be recognized by tips of fingers. you felt positions of
dots that formed letters and numbers. all over the world this
method of writing is still used on a high scale, That was a
gift from me to you, Mr. Louis Braille.

Wishful Imagination

I remember gettn instantly vexed when I heard the sound of crackn from my pyrex because that was the sound of what could be a whole re loss.

Sometimes it cracked but stood intact and i was able to transfer to another proctor, sometimes it shattered leaving oil all over, me take a loss, nope never, i waited till that shit dried, bagged it then hit the ave, i'll make most of my money back, i just had to deal with complaints of stems getting clogged by glass.

I had a one track mind, that was to lap competition and stay ahead on the grind. inf learned the game from coders, I took it further, trademarked a color and organized a team with ranks of power impressing my forefathers.

Poverty took me on one hell of trip, hunger fueled my flips to reach a brick, eventually my chauffeur became pain, i was driven by hurt, i couldn't let my deceased soldier's names die in vain.

the road was a bloody one, no stop signs, everyone was on go, road rage was daily, unfortunately i had to throw flowers for the dead over caskets due to altercations of boy and girl traffic.

There were a lot of windowpane tears, there were a lot of widow pain tears, I can hydroplane on all the tears shed for my peers throughout the years. i can make a slip and slide on randall, from castle hill to olmstead if i would've contained all the blood from those who are no longer here.

Getting drugs was easy, getting guns was easy, getting money was easy, it was all so simple man. gold, diamonds and tuning german engines was all basic fam, knock knock, who is it? telling the people on the opposite side of the door that they'll never see their loved one again was never part of the plan.

I did it again and again, at the start this wasn't what was envisioned at the end, I guess it's because we were just kids at that time mixing hope with wishful imaginations.

The Ultimate Surgeon

I'm awake in the state of shock, my motor skills are not working, can't move can't speak, all I have is my vision. I'm looking at each incision, the faces are right over me, yet I hear them as if there distant, I strain to listen. Pricks, cuts, tubes, flush after flush, lead and blood don't mix. They xray my chest.. Zap zap.. Bring the results ASAP! They ring the alarm, he has a entry and an exit, we didn't see the reentry hole in his armpit. The e r docs are numb, oh my god look how close it is to his lung, I hope his mom is on her way, today she might loose her son. My heart is still beating, the machines are still beeping, my wounds are still bleeding, who's the new face I'm seeing? A new doc on the surgery team? he's guiding them on how to make the internal bleeding stop, it's no longer a race of the clock, my body formed necessary clots. I'm to weak to even blink I close my eyes and go to sleep..hours pass... Im awake! Cheers and lots of hands shakes, to the doctors all the credit given, I thank them all as well, all except for one I don't see him here.... So when I get there, I'll personally thank my father who rest in heaven

Michelle
Joan
Barulich

Michelle Joan Barulich was born in Honolulu, Hawaii on the island of Oahu. She started writing poetry and songs with her younger brother Paul. They have written many songs in their teen years. She is currently studying Alternative Medicine and would like to become a Homeopathic Doctor. Michelle loves all kinds of animals and birds; she does wild rehabilitation. She has also rescued rock pigeons that make great pets.

https://www.facebook.com/michelle.barulich

Louis Dear

Louis was a young inventor.

His determination was impressive

He helped people and children to read

Who could not see

He opened a new world to them

He also made it possible for them to appreciate the sounds

of music too

What a great treasure you invented

Your legacy lives on.

A Sign

Standing alone on the edge of our destiny
Am I alone?
With an invisible hold on me
Why does everything have to die and fade away?

Here is my plead
Please show me the way
Hand me the key
So I can turn this destiny around
Hear my screams in my head
Please silent the echo of my tears
Lighten the pain
From my grieving heart
and now everything has to die and fade away

Standing alone on athe edge of our destiny
am I alone in this world filled with misery?
and now everything hasd to die and fade away

Show me a sign
So I can unlock the mysteries
Hear my plea
Sing to me
The answers that I seek
Talk sweetly and show me the way
and now everything has to die and fade away.

Cold

I walk down this lonely road
And the grounds pavement hits me too hard
Because without your love
I can't seem to go on

Cause its cold
without you
While the world keeps turning around
It keeps spinning too fast for me
Cold, without you

While the rain keeps coming around
And turns of the seasons
bring me down

Well, lately I've been pullin down the shades for my
privacy
I couldn't feel the warmth
projecting onto me
And I remember when life was filled with intimacy.

Now it's cold
cause without your love
is there reason to go on?
when it's cold
without your love.

Eliza Segiet

Eliza Segiet graduated with a Master's Degree in Philosophy at Jagiellonian University.
Received *Global Literature Guardian Award* – from Motivational Strips, World Nations

Writers' Union and Union Hispanomundial De Escritores (UHE) 2018.

Nominated for the Pushcart Prize 2019, 2021.

Laureate *Naji Naaman Literary Prize 2020*, *International Award Paragon of Hope* (2020),

World Award 2020 *Cesar Vallejo* for Literary Excellence.

Laureate of the Special Jury *Sahitto International Award* 2021, World Award *Premiul Fănuș Neagu* 2021.

Finalist *Golden Aster Book* World Literary Prize 2020, *Mili Dueli* 2022, Voci nel deserto 2022.

At the international Festival of Poetry CAMPIONATO MONDIALE DI POESIA (2021/2022) she won the title of vice-champion of the world.

Award BHARAT RATNA RABINDRANATH TAGORE INTERNATIONAL AWARD (2022).

Light
To the memory of Louis Braille

Between what
is visible for them
and what
they can see by touch
are dots
– the way to experience the world.

The magical alphabet
allowed
the touch to reach the Universe,
to become a paradise
cutting through the darkness to light.

The perforated sheet
bursts with possibilities
– to learn
– to experience
– to communicate.

They live more fully now
thanks to the Blind Man
who did not give up his dreams
– from the depths of darkness,
he brought out light.

Translated by Dorota Stępińska

Prosthesis

It used to be different.

Better?

More interesting!

There were faces,
not avatars.

Conversation
– not letters on the screen.

Words had the color of the voice
or the smell of print.

We didn't take for granted
being connected with the world.

Grandpa, what are you talking about?

I said it wrong
– today the phone is the extension of the hand

– the prosthesis of the present.

Translated by Artur Komoter

Web

The offline time
had a different measurement.

Condemned to loneliness on the Web,
they try
to find understanding
with people sometimes even without faces.
Just a few nice sentences,
enough to increase confidence in

– a woman?
– a man?
– the written words?

Condemned to loneliness on the Web,
they believe what they see on the screen.

Clicking –
I am not a robot
– is the only identity check.

Where are the moments
where without machines

– a Human understood a Human?

Translated by Artur Komoter

William S. Peters Sr.

Bill's writing career spans a period of over 50 years. Being first Published in 1972, Bill has since went on to Author in excess of 50 additional Volumes of Poetry, Short Stories, etc., expressing his thoughts on matters of the Heart, Spirit, Consciousness and Humanity. His primary focus is that of Love, Peace and Understanding!

Bill says . . .

I have always likened Life to that of a Garden. So, for me, Life is simply about the Seeds we Sow and Nourish. All things we "Think and Do", will "Be" Cause and eventually manifest itself to being an "Effect" within our own personal "Existences" and "Experiences" . . . whether it be Fruit, Flowers, Weeds or Barren Landscapes! Bill highly regards the Fruits of his Labor and wishes that everyone would thus go on to plant "Lovely" Seeds on "Good Ground" in their own Gardens of Life!

to connect with Bill, he is all things Inner Child

www.iaminnerchild.com

Personal Web Site

www.iamjustbill.com

Louis Braille

I turn dots to knowledge
Bumps on the paper to explorations
For he or she
Who wishes to travel

I cater to the blind
And some understand,
But there are far more
Who have eyes
And can not see

Mesmerized

At the top of the tallest mountains
Where the clouds kiss its peak
There belies a serene beauty
That few may ever speak

The beauty of nature
And the story it tells
Upon the common-mans soul
Casts her spells

No matter the seasons
Nor the time of day
If we but listen
Mother has much to say

She speaks of our nurturing
And our overall well being
But we are blinded children
Whose eyes are not seeing

We dance upon the precipice
Of our own demise
Ignoring our bond
And our creation's ties

We exist in a world
False-founded in delusion
And are content to continue
With our conjured confusion

But know ye this dear man
This way endureth not long
And son the day come
That ends our false song

The wind shall blow fiercely
Seeking Mother's retribution
For which man's conventions
Has not a solution

Yet we aimlessly meander
Down our errant path
Realizing in the end
Mother was all that we hath

In the meantime we also
Rail against each other
Connections be damned
Be it Sister, Father, Mother or Brother

We are mesmerized in full
Euphorically deludedly absolute
That no thing even Mother
Can not correct nor refute

We are the lost children
Seeking false bliss
When at the top of the mountain
Awaits pour blissful kiss

Look to the clouds
And the mountains as well
And silently listen
To the story they tell

The Gift

Today is a gift . . .

Who knows what tomorrow holds?
Should we live to see it,
It is a gift!

Should we see what is to be seen,
It is a gift!

Should we understand
What it is we saw
It is a gift!

Should we learn from
What was seen,
It is a gift!

Should we tell others of
What we have learned,
It is a gift to others.

Should they hear, listen and learn,
That is their gift.

Should they pay it forward
That is a gift
With no end.

Gifts are for giving! ~ wsp

The more gifts you give, the more gifts you receive.

William S. Peters, Sr.

The Butterfly Effect

"IS" in effect

May

2023

Featured Poets

~ * ~

Csp Shrivastava

Michael Lee Johnson

Taghrid Bou Merhi

Yasmin Brown

i Fly

because I Can

. . . said the Dreamer to the world.

www.iamjustbill.com

Csp
Shrivastava

Csp Shrivastava who resides in Bengaluru, India, is a bilingual poet (Hindi and English). His poems have been published in several national and international anthologies. He loves and cares for the human values and views literature as a continuous effort to understand the intricacies of the human psyche and nature.

A catastrophe in the offing...

Ingrained already in our psyche
Is happening of such a catastrophe

Are we heading to one such now
Unaware was no recourse somehow

The fast changing patterns of climate
Hastening of environs to the ultimate

A gift so rare that we got thro' ages
Deterioration now setting in which razes

A thoughtless vision sans precision
Vying n trying to fence their reason

The mad chasing of the whole race
Put shame to the face of grace

We enjoyed since yon n eons
Civilizations grew with grace

So long ignorance was bliss...
We were caught unaware n amiss

Awareness of the pinch prime
Alone can salvage the climatic decline

Now that the pinch is to the fore
How can we afford to ignore

Retracing our steps apace
Seems to be the only solace

The best of minds to rise up in tandem
To put to strict action n not at random.

Disgrace ~writ large

Melting ice, flashing floods
Earthquakes, cyclonic storms
Forest fires and draughts
All across the world
Writ large on our planet 's face!
So abrupt and quick —

Though, we know
Climate change -
As a phenomenon
A natural cycle of earth
Baffling is its hastening
Causing global warming
As backlash of human Deeds(misdeeds)!!!

Industrialisation in its wake
Urbanisation in its take

All for economic gains
Deforestation and rains

We are devoid of trees,
A destruction of Nature

With nuclear and military exercises
The likely extinction never ceases

Restoration of balance of Nature
Is the need of our stature

Away from the causes of pollution
Afforestation n awareness
Are bound to contribute
Towards a positive reverberation

A concerted wisdom

The Heritage, we boast of now
Had hidden bounties

The jungles, rivers n mountains
Abounding in nature's purity

Gone are their magnanimity

The other day only, heard of a death of climatic
immensities

The world aggregating thro' numerous vows n treaties
Land up in complex agonies

There commitments of measures
Such as lesser carbon emissions

Even garbage managing
And many a sundry factors damaging

It's all simply a prolonging strategies
Forgetting we lost several centuries

The wiser now are assets of lost kingdom
Hope lies in a really concerted wisdom.

Let's then, be up n doing
For changing our way of life...
Struggling, striving n surviving.

Michael
Lee
Johnson

Michael Lee Johnson is an internationally published poet in 44 countries, has several published poetry books, has been nominated for 6 Pushcart Prize awards, and 6 Best of the Net nominations.

I Age

Arthritis and aging make it hard,
I walk gingerly, with a cane, and walk
slow, bent forward, fear threats,
falls, fear denouement—
I turn pages, my family albums
become a task.
But I can still bake and shake,
sugar cookies, sweet potato,
lemon meringue pies.
Alone, most of my time,
but never on Sundays,
friends and communion,
United Church of Canada.
I chug a few down,
love my Blonde Canadian Pale Ale,
Copenhagen long cut a pinch of snuff.
I can still dance the Boogie-woogie,
Lindy Hop in my living room,
with my nursing care home partner.
Aging has left me with youthful dimples,
but few long-term promises.

Crypt in the Sky

Order me up,
no one knows
where this crypt in the sky
like a condo on the 5th floor
suite don't sell me out
over the years;
please don't bury me beneath
this ground, don't let me decay
inside my time pine casket.
Don't let me burn to cremate
skull last to turn to ashes.
Treasure me high where no one goes,
no arms reach, stretch.
Building for the Centuries
then just let it fall.
These few precious dry bones
preserved for you, sealed in the cloud
no relocation is necessary,
no flowers need to be planted,
no dusting off that dust each year,
no sinners can reach this high.
Jesus' heaven, Jesus' sky.

Note: *Dedicated to the passing of beloved Katie Balaskas.*

Priscilla, Let's Dance

Priscilla, Puerto Rican songbird,
an island jungle dancer, Cuban heritage,
rare parrot, a singer survivor near extinction.
She sounds off on notes, music her
vocals hearing background bongos,
piano keys, Cuban horns.
Quote the verse patterns,
quilt the pieces skirt bleeds,
then blend colors to light a tropical prism.
Steamy Salsa, a little twist, cha-cha-cha
dancing rhythms of passions, sacred these islands.
Everything she has is movement
tucked nice and tight but explosive.
She mimics these ancient sounds
showing her ribs, her naked body.
Her ex-lovers remain nightmares
pointed daggers, so criminal, so stereotyped.
Priscilla purifies her dreams with repentance.
She pours her heart out, everything
condensed to the bone, petite boobies,
cheap bras, flamboyant Gi strings.
Her vocabulary is that of sin and Catholicism.
Island hurricanes form her own Jesus
slants of hail, detonate thunder,
the collapse of hell in her hands after midnight.
Priscilla remains a background rabble-rouser,
almost remorseful, no apologies
to the counsel of Judas
wherever he hangs.

Taghrid Bou Merhi

Taghrid Bou Merhi is a Lebanese poetess, writer, and translator living in Brazil. She holds a Law degree and is ambassador of the team "International Cultural Salon Association"and ambassador of Brazil in the American P.L.O.T.S. Magazin and ambassador of Lebanon in the Association of the World Union of Writers and Artists UMEA Portugal . Member of prestigious platform Of WWWU World Nations Writers' Union Kazakhstan. She is an advisor to the countries Al-Sham literary platform for literary translation. Brand Ambassador from Brazil for Moncheri Escapes - a leading travel agency in India.She won the Nizar Sartawi International Translator Award for Creativity 2021 in the field of translation and literature.She won the 2nd Annual Zhengxin International Poet Award 2022.She hon received the World Prize Prestigious "RAHIM KARIM WORLD PRIZE".

Editor of Al-Arabe Today, Rainbow,Agharid, Al-Nil Walfurat, Literária and Allaylak Magazine.Fluent in Arabic (native language), French, English, Portuguese, Italian and Spanish.Her poems have been published in numerous international anthologies‹various Literary magazines,journals and websites.Her poems have been translated into more than 33 languages.
Her books include: 1. Songs of longing; 2.The Keys of Science:Verses and Manifestations; 3. Philosophies at the Edge of the Soul; 4. Flowers Of Love; 5. Wounds of the heart; 6. La Esperanza; 7. Mine Is Not Mine ; 8. Falling Alphabet.

I Need Your Voice!

I need your voice to speak with,
But the wind is lavish
And the sea is mute.
I am splintered
My wound is deep
I am torn apart
And my whole is burning
Oh how I am shrouded in pain,
And is there but pain for who is full of longing
Like a stormy night fed up with the madness of rain
So Cut with your waves
For The wound will set you free
And Don't break the foam sleeping in my lungs
Because between the sea of longing and this wound is a
pact
Has your voice become ink
So I can pledge allegiance to it?!
Behind the madness of sea, lovers are walking!
Oh eyelid of my heart!
And these thorns are slapping it
Oh water sadness and silenced fire,
Is this endeavor a failure?
Silence ignites in the body of the poem
Dances with the clouds
Spins and spins
And your voice is like a harp
I wished it vocalised !!!

Like Waiting!!

Since you have cut the ropes of sleep, while you are
waiting for your own self
Go flow from you to yourself!
Like a secret blood just drawn from the bank of time.
Oh displaced person to amputated places, while your
eyelids shed from departure, sadness drops from the sweat
of the sky sixty graves.
While you wait for yourself
Think of the children of death and the fires that burn.
You should have died in order for us to sleep.
You should have eaten the fire ignited from your waiting
So you can expel your pain and render it to ashes.
Die slowly when you come out of yourself
Like a bouquet of flowers turned yellow, so I can feel the
alienation and the empty loneliness.
The bird that slumbered on a paper kite, stopped wailing on
electricity poles.
The heads of passers-by were giving him a fleeting look.
And a crazy camera stands in the middle of the road:" Oh
my helplessness"!.
Oh air cut from the paper of time
There are tricks that failed to cross
There are hands that erase in ink the face of sorrows.
Oh traveller..!
When you get tired of leaning on a cane waiting for
yourself
Remember that you are still breathing in the midst of this
fire
Due to your five daily prayers!.

Alone On The Edge Of The Night!

I have never seen him alone sitting on the edge of the night
Reducing his thoughts of sadness and pain.
Time as life
Both lead you to a point in the palm of the hand
They hug together for fear of a boring session.
The earth wished that it could swallow his grief
But it happened that today is a holiday, and the sea is on a
long vacation.
I had to wait in the midst of the planets
Hoping the sign of fortune would smile without the monitor
cameras following us.
I have never seen him, before the ideals collapsed...
He fabricated a double excuse, turned his shadow to pass
through
And bent down a little to drag a picture resting on a wall.
The places were sleeping on both ends of the road
And just his bowed back, helplessly, passed by me bleakly
and silently.
I pretended to be staring at the sky
Wishing he would shoot his rope of silence
So he would die, and we can both survive together.
That night, i was crying and wailing.
That night,
He deserted the surface of his image, far away from the
screams of his pain and loneliness.
That night,
I found a reason to love the pictures that the night presents
for the homeless.
And in one of these back places, i saw the whole of him
Half of it is stuck there and the other half is determined to
stay together.

Yasmin
Brown

Yasmin Brown is an author and Healing Centered Life Coach on a mission to empower women. As a women's mental health advocate Yasmin engages through literacy and creative expression. She is a best-selling co-author of *Voices of the 21st Century Resilient Women Who Rise and Make a Difference* in addition to publishing several other books such as *I Just Want to be Normal, The Iced Tea of Friendship, The Silent Destruction* and more.

Ms. Brown is also featured in Soul Pitt Magazine for her first book *The Silent Destruction in addition to Shoutout Atlanta, RGP Muse and Intellectual Inc.*

Mirror, Mirror

Mirror, Mirror what do you see
I see unbearable pain and damage staring back at me.
All the times I cried, feeling like I died
When I close my eyes,
Darkness runs rampant inside.
Deeming the brightness I hide.
Shining light I cannot see
Bright lights whispering back to me.
I open your eyes,
Listening to the voice inside.
You brave, courageous young woman….tenacious and contagious
Your power and strength
Truly meant to be spontaneous.
Your purpose, your journey—powerful and influential.
Now shine bright to the sky… Guide your eyes
looking at my reflection with a sigh.
Mirror, Mirror
I want to see
My authentic reflection in acceptance of me.

Smile

The versatility of a smile may only last for a while
A while of happiness
A while of pain
Masquerading expressions so you do not go insane
Insane with emotion of simple bliss covering feelings of pain
Pain trying to change the past while missing the future
The future is now
Devote now to see the beauty with thee—Smile
Smile to see the message within me
The message to relax
Relax it is okay
Okay to feel emotions
Emotions with a smile, even if it is only for a while
So, Smile

A Woman's Faith

A woman's faith is steadfast in the word
The word of God
I am strong
I am courageous
I am the child of God
The affirmation of strength
Strength to endure
Just once more
To pray the impossible
The faith of possibilities
Possibilities, no weapon formed against me shall prosper
Prosperity to order, order her steps
Steps to succeed and plan not to fail
Planting seeds to grow
Grow in faith and love
Loving thy neighbor as yourself
Allowing yourself to feel weeping if only for a night
The night A Woman's Faith finds joy in the morning light.

Remembering

our fallen soldiers of verse

Janet Perkins Caldwell

February 14, 1959 ~ September 20, 2016

Alan W. Jankowski

16 March 1961 ~ 10 March 2017

Inner Child Press

News

Published Books

by

Poetry Posse Members

We are so excited to share and announce a few of the current books, as well as the new and upcoming books of some of our Poetry Posse authors.

On the following pages we present to you ...

Alicja Maria Kuberska

Jackie Davis Allen

Gail Weston Shazor

hülya n. yılmaz

Nizar Sartawi

Elizabeth E. Castillo

Faleeha Hassan

Fahredin Shehu

Kimberly Burnham

Caroline 'Ceri' Nazareno

Eliza Segiet

Teresa E. Gallion

William S. Peters, Sr.

Now Available

www.innerchildpress.com

Once upon a Time

in

Turkey

hülya n. yılmaz

Now Available
www.innerchildpress.com

Unapologetically

BLACK

&

Blues

william s. peters, sr.

Now Available
www.innerchildpress.com

Pulling Coats

Shareef Abdur-Rasheed

Now Available
www.innerchildpress.com

147

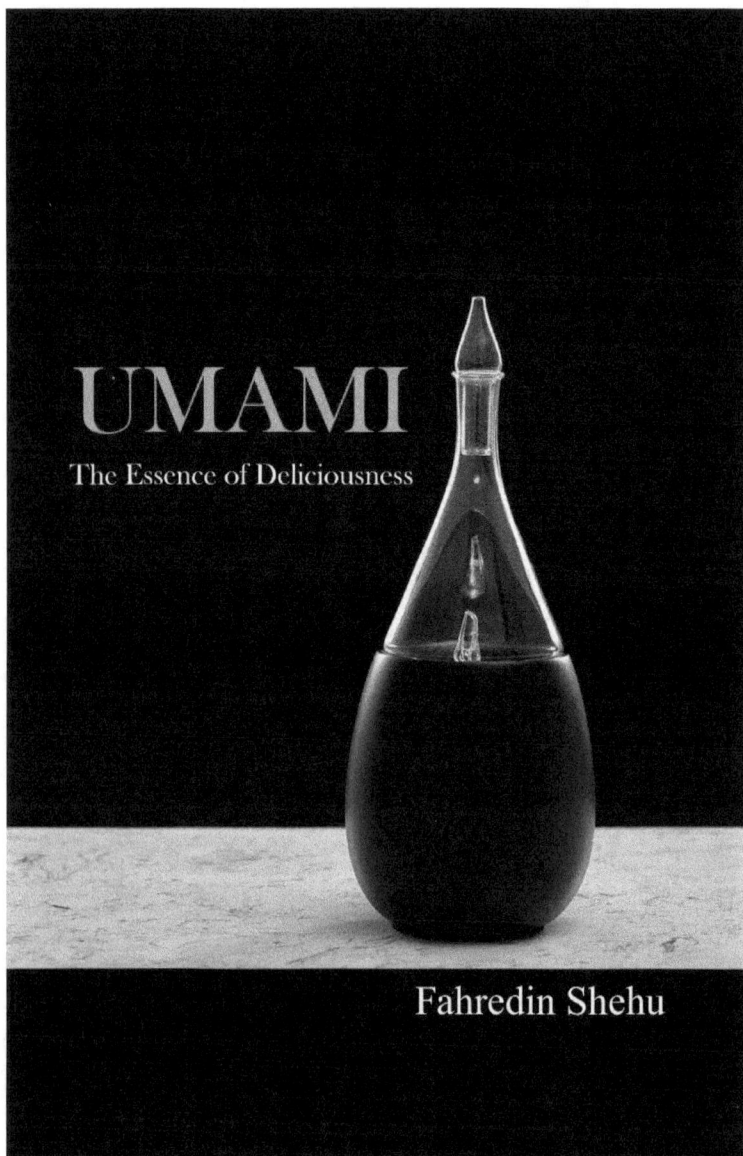

UMAMI
The Essence of Deliciousness

Fahredin Shehu

Now Available
www.innerchildpress.com

After the Frost

Alicja Maria Kuberska

Now Available

www.innerchildpress.com

Fahredin Shehu

ORMUS

Now Available
www.innerchildpress.com

Ahead of My Time

...from the Streets to the Stages

Albert 'Infinite' Carrasco

Now Available

www.innerchildpress.com

Eliza Segiet

To Be More

Now Available at
www.amazon.com/gp/product/B08MYL5B7S/ref=
dbs_a_def_rwt_hsch_vapi_tkin_p1_i2

SEARCH FOR THE MAGICAL MULTILINGUAL FROG

A Tale of Ribbit in 50 Languages

KIMBERLY BURNHAM

Now Available at
www.innerchildpress.com

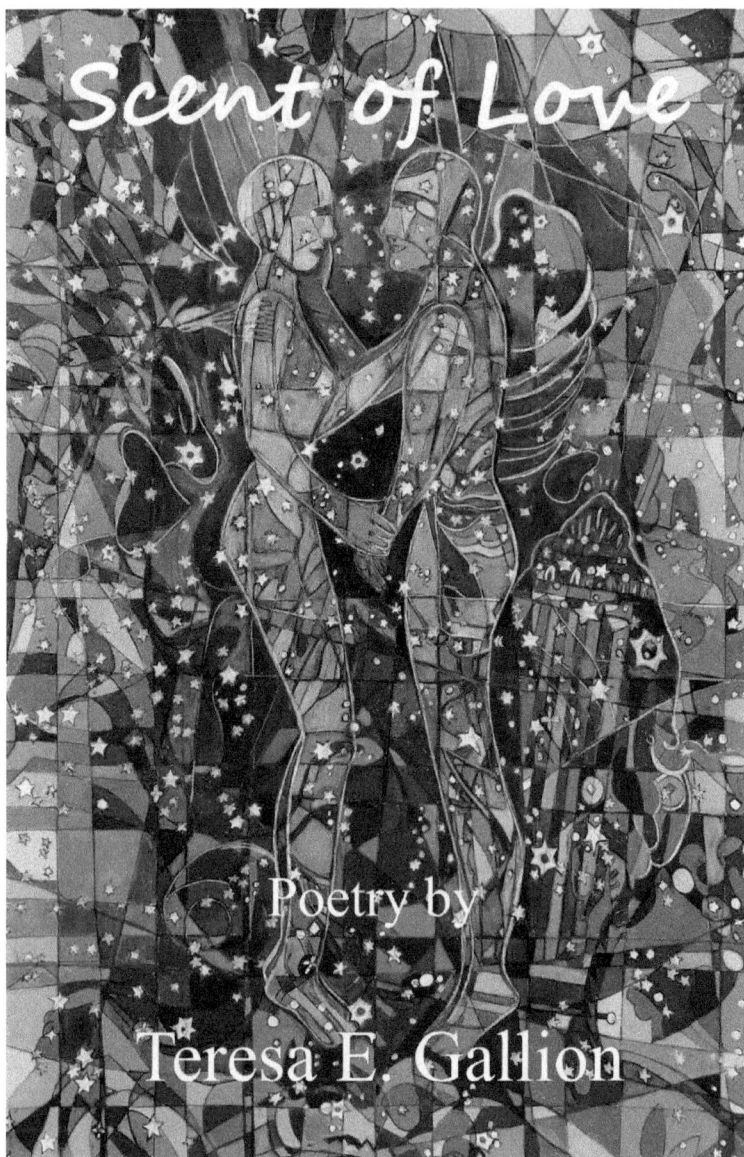

Scent of Love

Poetry by

Teresa E. Gallion

Now Available

www.innerchildpress.com

Inner Reflections
of the
Muse

Elizabeth Castillo

Now Available

www.innerchildpress.com

Letter - Poems

from a Beloved

hülya n. yılmaz

Now Available

www.innerchildpress.com

Now Available

www.innerchildpress.com

COMING SOON
www.innerchildpress.com

The Book of krisar

volume v

william s. peters, sr.

Now Available

www.innerchildpress.com

The Book of krisar

Volume I

william s. peters, sr.

The Book of krisar

Volume II

william s. peters, sr.

Now Available

www.innerchildpress.com

The Book of krisar

Volume III

william s. peters, sr.

The Book of krisar

Volume IV

william s. peters, sr.

Now Available
www.innerchildpress.com

Velvet Passions

of

Calibrated Quarks

Caroline Nazareno-Gabis

Now Available

www.innerchildpress.com

Unpaired

Eliza Segiet

Translated by Artur Komoter

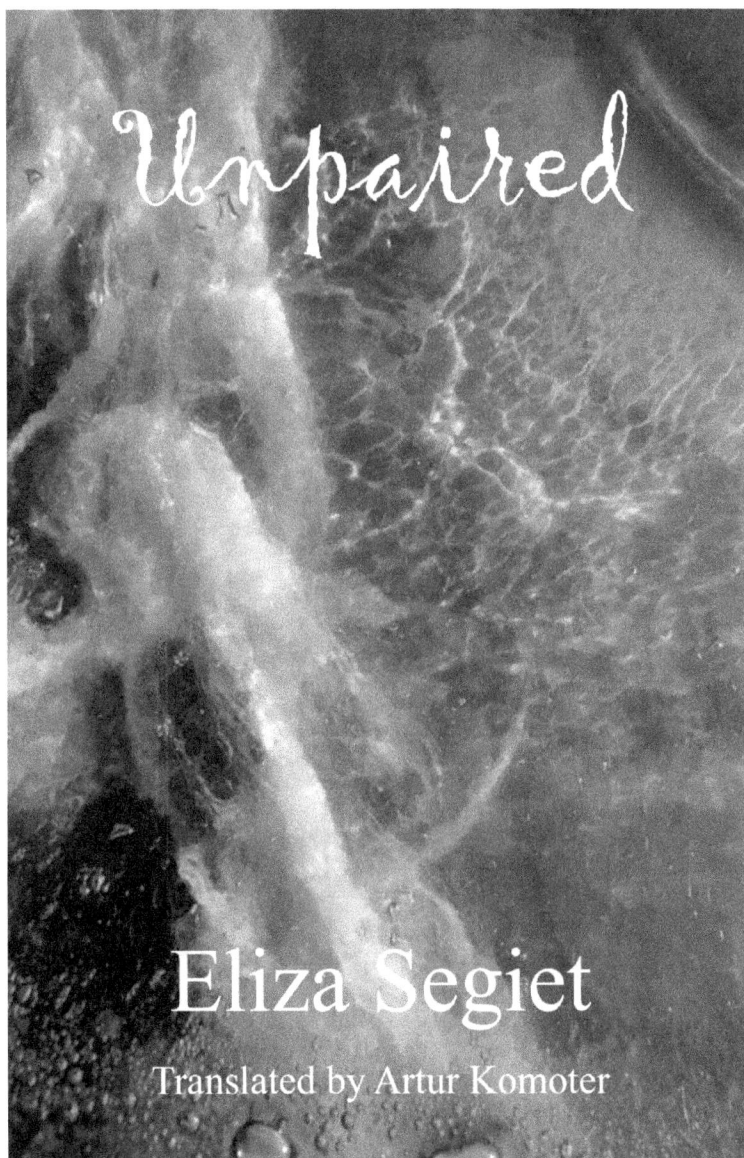

Private Issue

www.innerchildpress.com

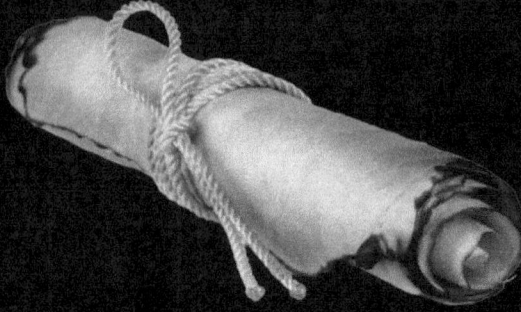

Canlarım

My Lifeblood

poetry in Turkish and English

hülya n. yılmaz

Now Available

www.innerchildpress.com

Butterfly's Voice

Faleeha Hassan

Translated by William M. Hutchins

Now Available at
www.innerchildpress.com

No Illusions

Through the Looking Glass

Jackie Davis Allen

Now Available at
www.innerchildpress.com

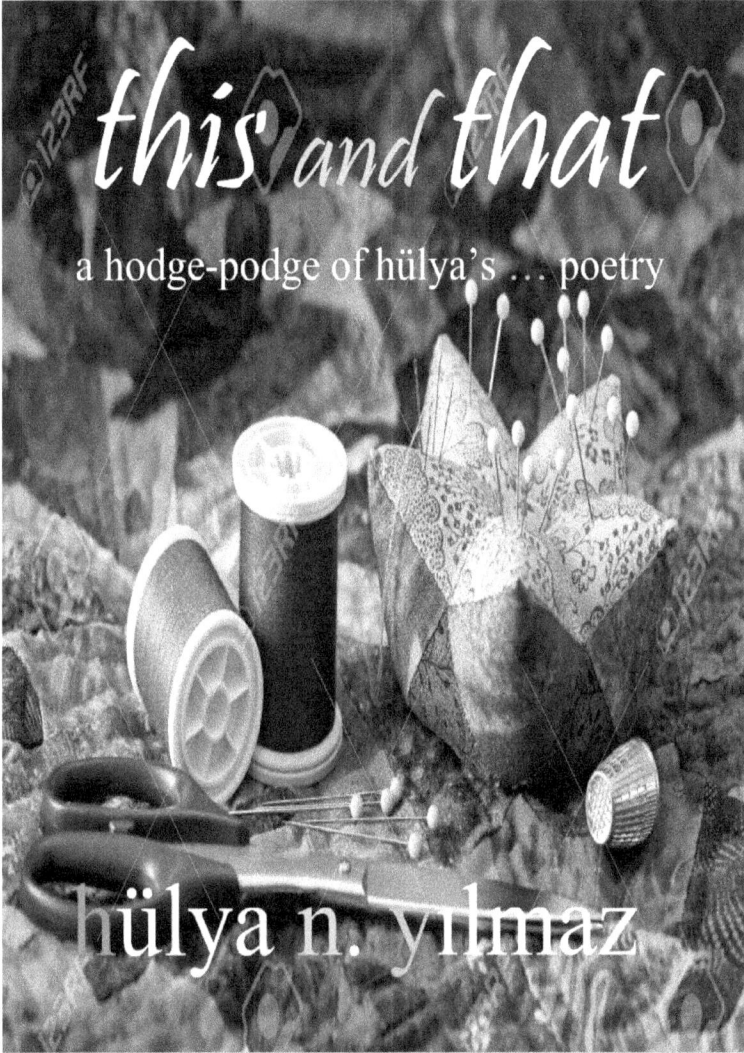

this and that

a hodge-podge of hülya's ... poetry

hülya n. yılmaz

Now Available at
www.innerchildpress.com

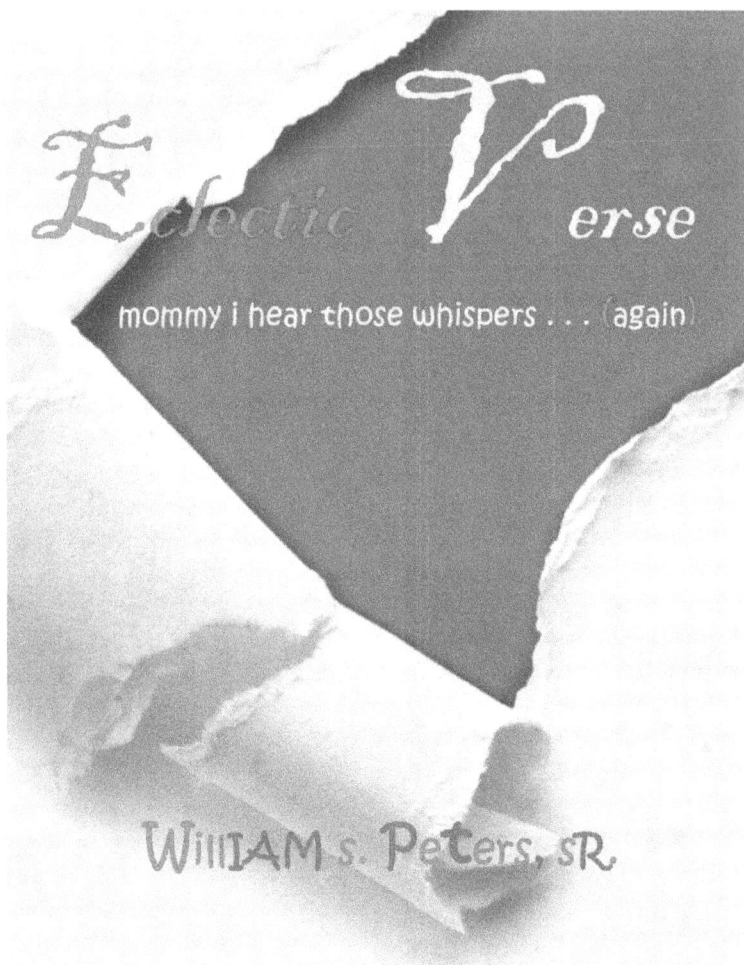

Eclectic Verse

mommy i hear those whispers . . . (again)

WilliAM s. PeTers, sR.

Now Available at
www.innerchildpress.com

HERENOW

FAHREDIN SHEHU

Now Available at
www.innerchildpress.com

Magnetic People

Eliza Segiet

Translated by Artur Komoter

Now Available at
www.innerchildpress.com

Dark Side
of the
Moon

Jackie Davis Allen

Now Available at
www.innerchildpress.com

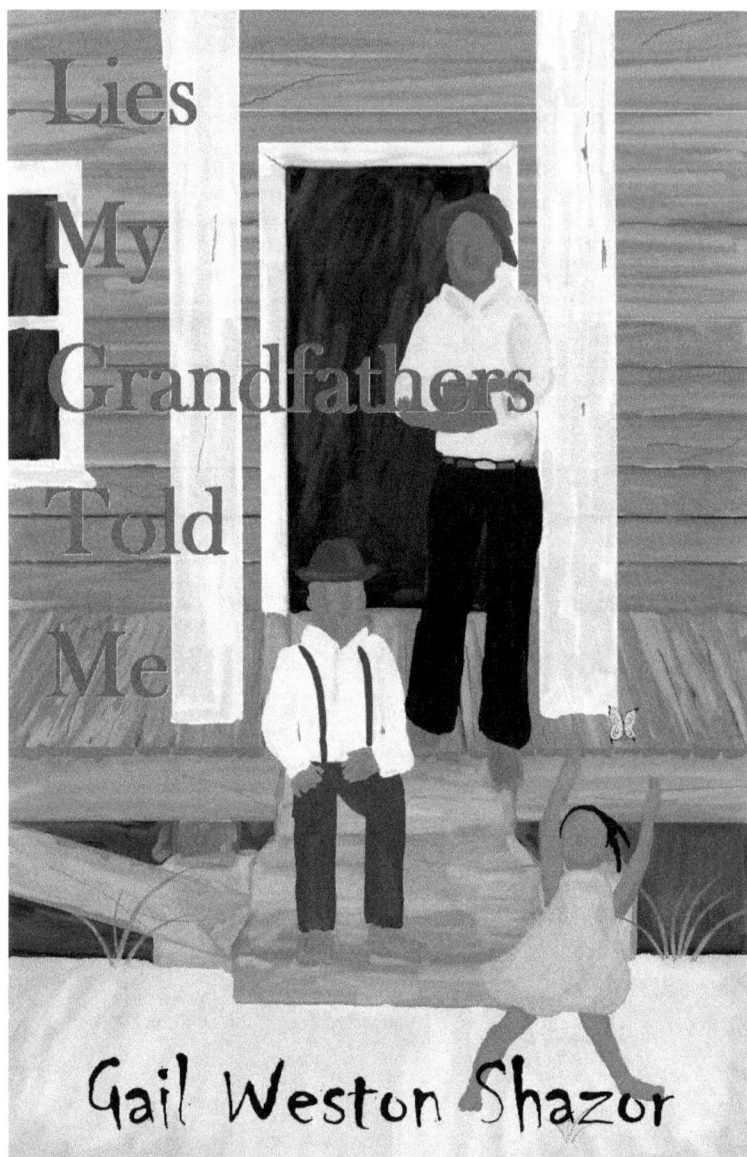

Lies My Grandfathers Told Me

Gail Weston Shazor

Now Available at
www.innerchildpress.com

Aflame

Memoirs in Verse

hülya n. yılmaz

Now Available at
www.innerchildpress.com

Mass Graves

Faleeha Hassan

Now Available at
www.innerchildpress.com

Breakfast

for

Butterflies

Faleeha Hassan

Now Available at

www.innerchildpress.com

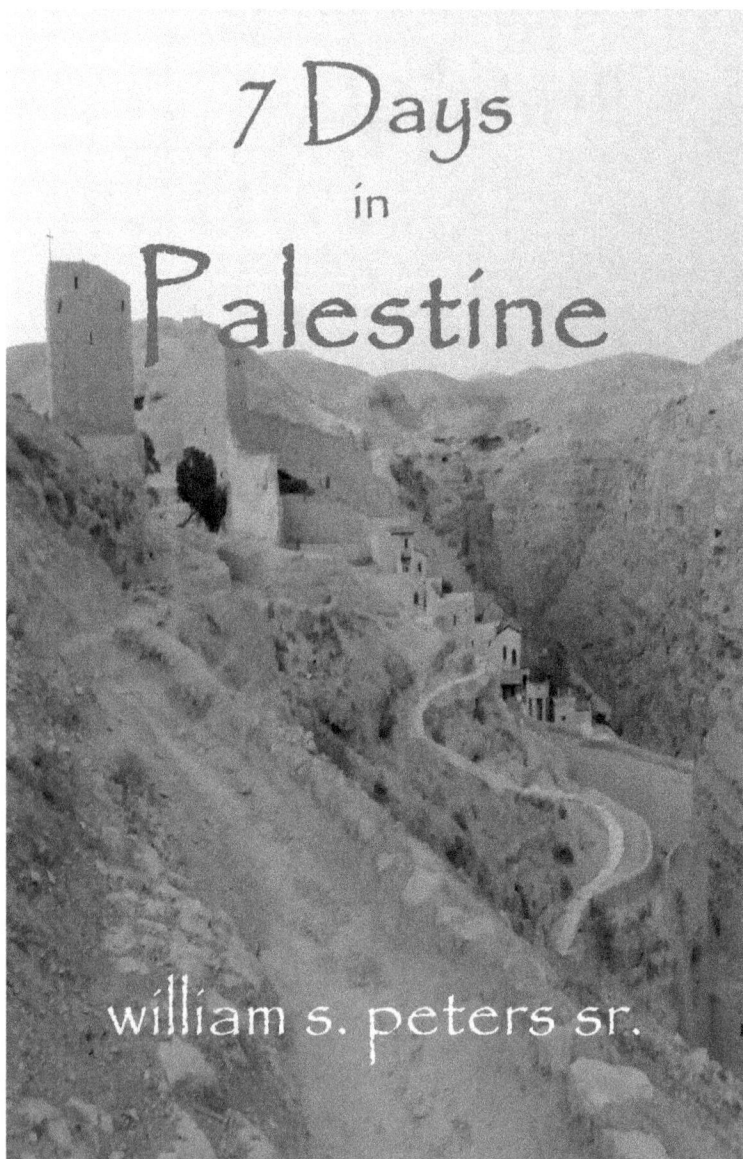

7 Days
in
Palestine

william s. peters sr.

Now Available at
www.innerchildpress.com

inner child press
presents

Tunisian Dreams

william s. peters, sr.

Now Available at
www.innerchildpress.com

INNER CHILD PRESS

THIS IS WHY I
SLEEP

william s. peters sr.

Now Available at

www.innerchildpress.com

Other

Anthological

works from

Inner Child Press International

www.innerchildpress.com

World Healing World Peace 2022
Poets for Humanity

Now Available

www.worldhealingworldpeacepoetry.com

World Healing World Peace
2020

Poets for Humanity

Now Available

www.worldhealingworldpeacepoetry.com

Now Available
www.innerchildpress.com

Inner Child Press International
&
The Year of the Poet
present

Poetry

the best of 2020

Poets of the World

Now Available

www.innerchildpress.com

Inner Child Press International

presents

W.A.R.

We Are Revolution

Poets for Humanity

Now Available
www.innerchildpress.com

the Heart of a Poet

words for a better tomorrow

The Conscious Poets

Now Available
www.innerchildpress.com

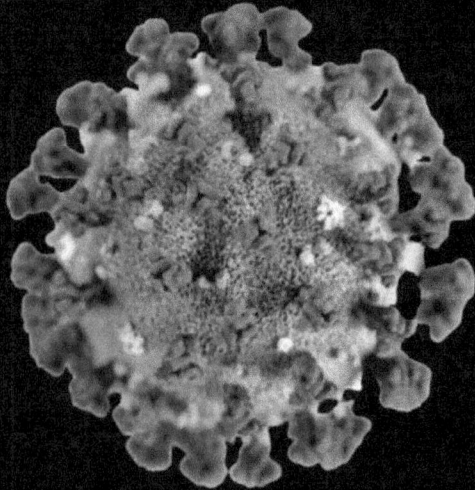

Corona

Social Distancing

Poets for Humanity

Now Available

www.innerchildpress.com

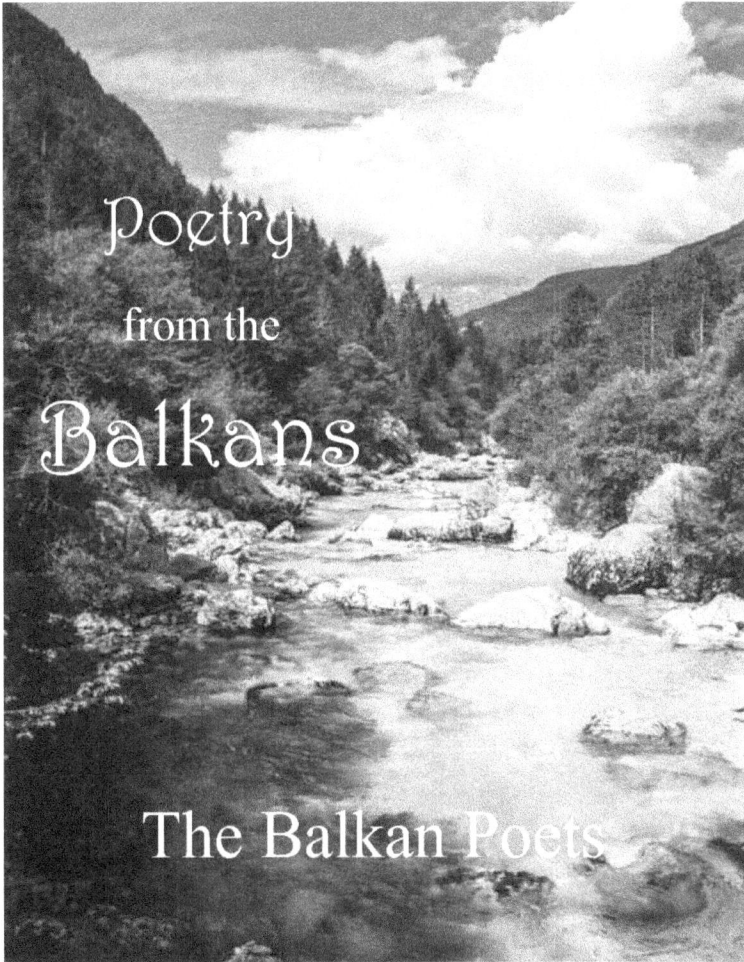

Now Available at
www.innerchildpress.com

Now Available at
www.innerchildpress.com

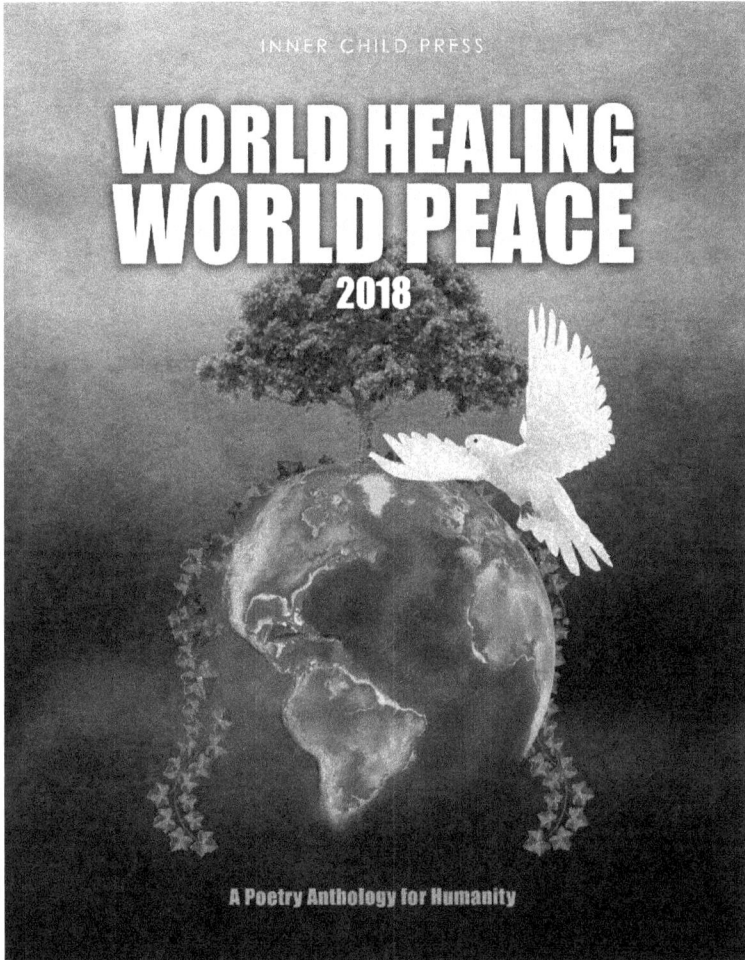

INNER CHILD PRESS

WORLD HEALING
WORLD PEACE
2018

A Poetry Anthology for Humanity

Now Available at
www.innerchildpress.com

Inner Child Press International
presents

𝔄 𝔏ove 𝔄nthology

2019

The Love Poets

Now Available

www.worldhealingworldpeacepoetry.com

INNER CHILD PRESS

WORLD HEALING
WORLD PEACE
2018

A Poetry Anthology for Humanity

Now Available

www.worldhealingworldpeacepoetry.com

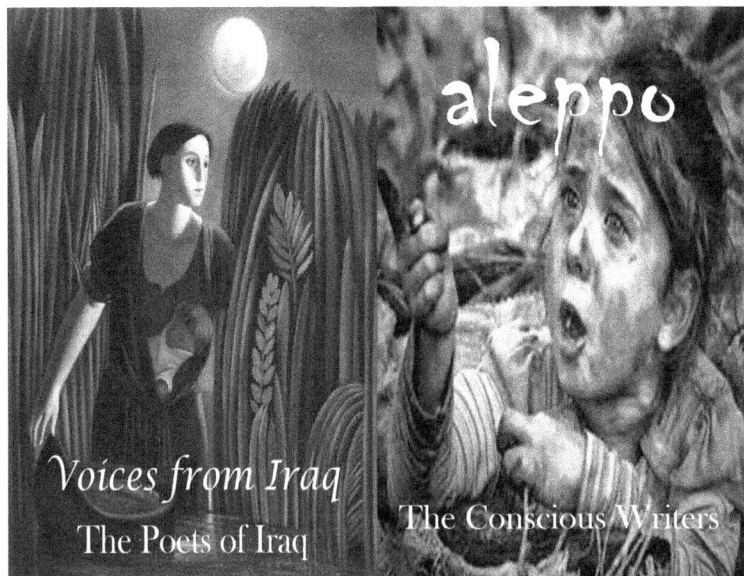

Now Available

www.innerchildpress.com/anthologies

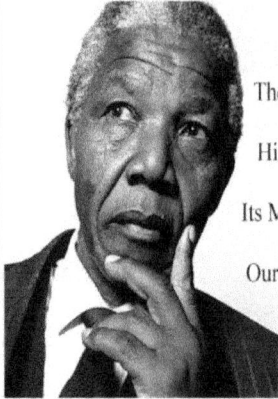

Mandela

The Man

His Life

Its Meaning

Our Words

Poetry . . . Commentary & Stories
The Anthological Writers

A GATHERING OF WORDS

POETRY & COMMENTARY
FOR

TRAYVON MARTIN

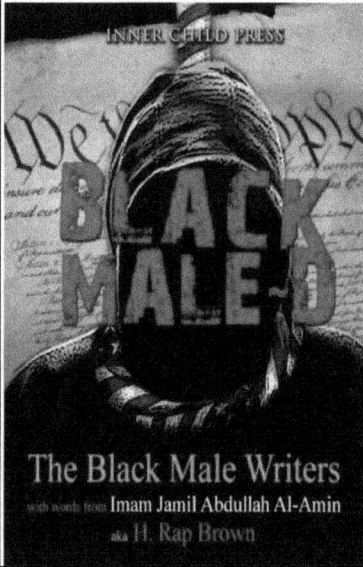

INNER CHILD PRESS

BLACK MALE-D

The Black Male Writers
with words from **Imam Jamil Abdullah Al-Amin**
aka H. Rap Brown

I
want
my
poetry
to... *volume* 4

the conscious poets
inspired by . . . Monte Smith

Now Available

Now Available

www.innerchildpress.com/anthologies

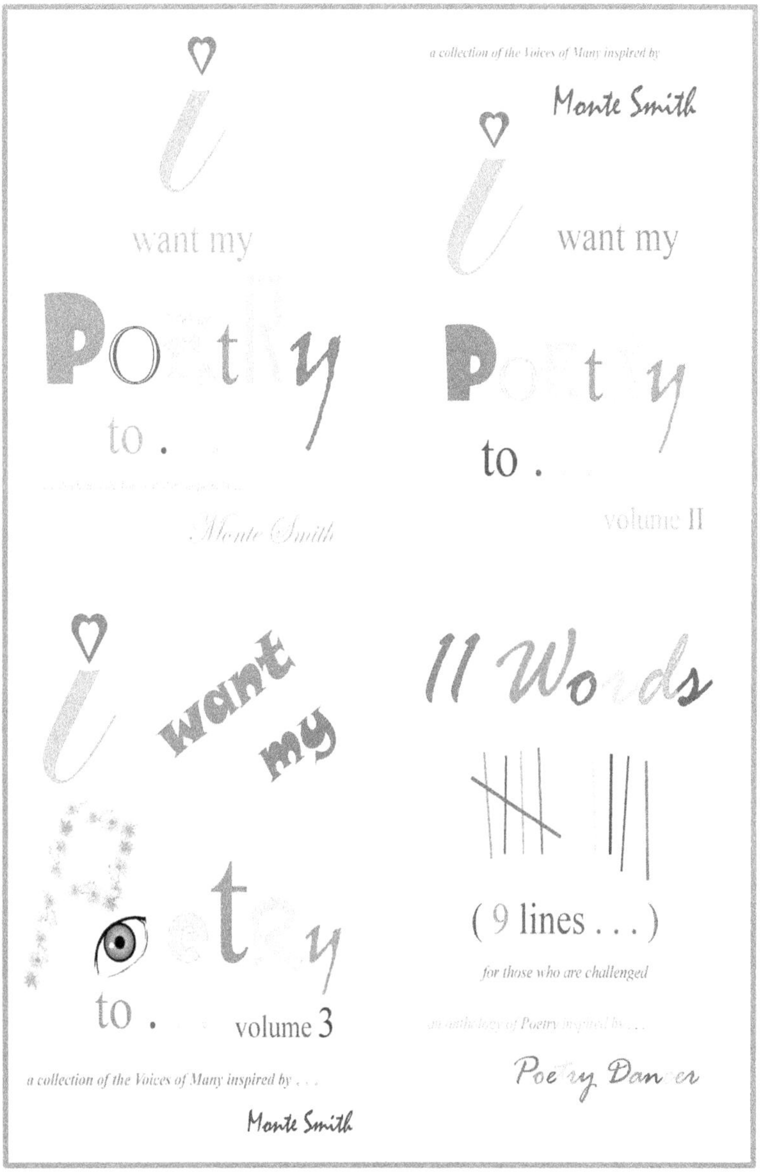

Now Available

www.innerchildpress.com/anthologies

The Year of the Poet
January 2014

The Poetry Posse

Jamie Bond
Gail Weston Shazor
Albert 'Infinite' Carrasco
Siddartha Beth Pierce
Janet P. Caldwell
June 'Bugg' Barefield
Debbie M. Allen
Tony Henninger
Joe DaVerbal Minddancer
Robert Gibbons
Neetu Wali
Shareef Abdur-Rasheed
William S. Peters, Sr.

Carnation

Our January Feature
Terri L. Johnson

the Year of the Poet
February 2014

violets

The Poetry Posse
Jamie Bond
Gail Weston Shazor
Albert 'Infinite' Carrasco
Siddartha Beth Pierce
Janet P. Caldwell
June 'Bugg' Barefield
Debbie M. Allen
Tony Henninger
Joe DaVerbal Minddancer
Robert Gibbons
Neetu Wali
Shareef Abdur-Rasheed
William S. Peters, Sr.

Our February Features
Teresa E. Gallion & Robert Gibson

the Year of the Poet
March 2014

The Poetry Posse
Jamie Bond
Gail Weston Shazor
Albert 'Infinite' Carrasco
Siddartha Beth Pierce
Janet P. Caldwell
June 'Bugg' Barefield
Debbie M. Allen
Tony Henninger
Joe DaVerbal Minddancer
Robert Gibbons
Neetu Wali
Shareef Abdur-Rasheed
Kimberly Burnham
William S. Peters, Sr.

daffodil

Our March Featured Poets
Alicia C. Cooper & hülya yılmaz

the Year of the Poet
April 2014

The Poetry Posse
Jamie Bond
Gail Weston Shazor
Albert 'Infinite' Carrasco
Siddartha Beth Pierce
Janet P. Caldwell
June 'Bugg' Barefield
Debbie M. Allen
Tony Henninger
Joe DaVerbal Minddancer
Robert Gibbons
Neetu Wali
Shareef Abdur-Rasheed
Kimberly Burnham
William S. Peters, Sr.

Our April Featured Poets
Fahredin Shehu
Martina Reisz Newberry
Justin Blackburn
Monte Smith

Sweet Pea

celebrating international poetry month

Now Available

www.innerchildpress.com/the-year-of-the-poet

200

Now Available

The Year of the Poet
September 2014

Aster   Morning-Glory

Wild Charm of September Birthday Flower

September Feature Poets
Florence Malone * Keith Alan Hamilton

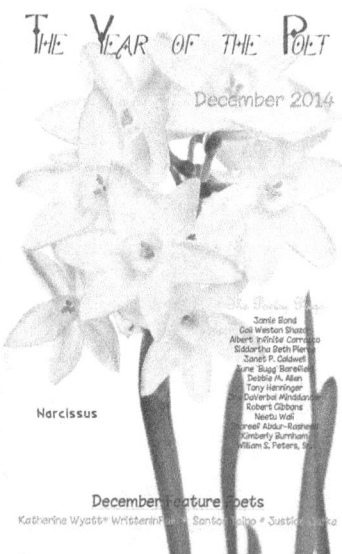

The Poetry Posse
Jamie Bond * Gail Weston Shazor * Albert Infinite Carrasco * Siddartha Beth Pierce
Janet P. Caldwell * June 'Bugg' Barefield * Debbie M. Allen * Tony Henninger
Joe DaVerbal Minddancer * Robert Gibbons * Neetu Wali * Shareef Abdur-Rasheed
Kimberly Burnham * William S. Peters, Sr.

THE YEAR OF THE POET
October 2014

Red Poppy

The Poetry Posse
Jamie Bond * Gail Weston Shazor * Albert Infinite Carrasco * Siddartha Beth Pierce
Janet P. Caldwell * June 'Bugg' Barefield * Debbie M. Allen * Tony Henninger
Joe DaVerbal Minddancer * Robert Gibbons * Neetu Wali * Shareef Abdur-Rasheed
Kimberly Burnham * William S. Peters, Sr.

October Feature Poets
Ceri Naz * Rajendra Padhi * Elizabeth Castillo

THE YEAR OF THE POET
November 2014

Chrysanthemum

The Poetry Posse
Jamie Bond * Gail Weston Shazor * Albert Infinite Carrasco * Siddartha Beth Pierce
Janet P. Caldwell * June 'Bugg' Barefield * Debbie M. Allen * Tony Henninger
Joe DaVerbal Minddancer * Robert Gibbons * Neetu Wali * Shareef Abdur-Rasheed
Kimberly Burnham * William S. Peters, Sr.

November Feature Poets
Jocelyn Mosman * Jackie Allen * James Moore * Neville Hiatt

THE YEAR OF THE POET
December 2014

Narcissus

Jamie Bond
Gail Weston Shazor
Albert Infinite Carrasco
Siddartha Beth Pierce
Janet P. Caldwell
June 'Bugg' Barefield
Debbie M. Allen
Tony Henninger
Joe DaVerbal Minddancer
Robert Gibbons
Neetu Wali
Shareef Abdur-Rasheed
Kimberly Burnham
William S. Peters, Sr.

December Feature Poets
Katherine Wyatt* WhisperinFire * Santosh Bishno * Justin Banks

Now Available
www.innerchildpress.com/the-year-of-the-poet

202

The Year of the Poet II — January 2015
Garnet
The Poetry Posse
Jamie Bond
Gail Weston Shazor
Albert 'Infinite' Carrasco
Siddartha Beth Pierce
Janet P. Caldwell
Tony Henninger
Joe DaVerbal Minddancer
Robert Gibbons
Neetu Wali
Shareef Abdur – Rasheed
Kimberly Burnham
Ann White
Keith Alan Hamilton
Katherine Wyatt
Fahredin Shehu
Hülya N. Yılmaz
Teresa E. Gallion
Jackie Allen
William S. Peters, Sr.
January Feature Poets
Bismay Mohanti * Jen Walls * Eric Judah

THE YEAR OF THE POET II — February 2015
Amethyst
THE POETRY POSSE
Jamie Bond
Gail Weston Shazor
Albert 'Infinite' Carrasco
Siddartha Beth Pierce
Janet P. Caldwell
Tony Henninger
Joe DaVerbal Minddancer
Robert Gibbons
Neetu Wali
Shareef Abdur – Rasheed
Kimberly Burnham
Ann White
Keith Alan Hamilton
Katherine Wyatt
Fahredin Shehu
Hülya N. Yılmaz
Teresa E. Gallion
Jackie Allen
William S. Peters, Sr.
FEBRUARY FEATURE POETS
Iram Fatima * Bob McNeil * Kerstin Centervall

The Year of the Poet II — March 2015
Our Featured Poets
Heung Sook * Anthony Arnold * Alicia Poland
Bloodstone
The Poetry Posse 2015
Jamie Bond * Gail Weston Shazor * Albert 'Infinite' Carrasco
Siddartha Beth Pierce * Janet P. Caldwell * Tony Henninger
Joe DaVerbal Minddancer * Neetu Wali * Shareef Abdur – Rasheed
Kimberly Burnham * Ann White * Keith Alan Hamilton
Katherine Wyatt * Fahredin Shehu * Hülya N. Yılmaz
Teresa E. Gallion * Jackie Allen * William S. Peters, Sr.

The Year of the Poet II — April 2015
Celebrating International Poetry Month
Our Featured Poets
Raja Williams * Dennis Ferado * Laure Charazac
Diamonds
The Poetry Posse 2015
Jamie Bond * Gail Weston Shazor * Albert 'Infinite' Carrasco
Siddartha Beth Pierce * Janet P. Caldwell * Tony Henninger
Joe DaVerbal Minddancer * Neetu Wali * Shareef Abdur – Rasheed
Kimberly Burnham * Ann White * Keith Alan Hamilton
Katherine Wyatt * Fahredin Shehu * Hülya N. Yılmaz
Teresa E. Gallion * Jackie Allen * William S. Peters, Sr.

Now Available

www.innerchildpress.com/the-year-of-the-poet

The Year of the Poet II
May 2015

May's Featured Poets

Geri Algeri
Akin Mosi Chimney
Anna Jakubczak

Emeralds

The Poetry Posse 2015
Jamie Bond * Gail Weston Shazor * Albert 'Infinite' Carrasco
Siddartha Beth Pierce * Janet P. Caldwell * Tony Henninger
Joe DaVerbal Minddancer * Neetu Wali * Shareef Abdur – Rasheed
Kimberly Burnham * Ann White * Keith Alan Hamilton
Katherine Wyatt * Fahredin Shehu * Hülya N. Yılmaz
Teresa E. Gallion * Jackie Allen * William S. Peters, Sr.

The Year of the Poet II
June 2015

June's Featured Poets

Anahit Arustamyan * Yvette D. Murrell * Regina A. Walker

Pearl

The Poetry Posse 2015
Jamie Bond * Gail Weston Shazor * Albert 'Infinite' Carrasco
Siddartha Beth Pierce * Janet P. Caldwell * Tony Henninger
Joe DaVerbal Minddancer * Neetu Wali * Shareef Abdur – Rasheed
Kimberly Burnham * Ann White * Keith Alan Hamilton
Katherine Wyatt * Fahredin Shehu * Hülya N. Yılmaz
Teresa E. Gallion * Jackie Allen * William S. Peters, Sr.

The Year of the Poet II
July 2015

The Featured Poets for July 2015

Abhik Shome * Christina Neal * Robert Neal

Rubies

The Poetry Posse 2015
Jamie Bond * Gail Weston Shazor * Albert 'Infinite' Carrasco
Siddartha Beth Pierce * Janet P. Caldwell * Tony Henninger
Joe DaVerbal Minddancer * Neetu Wali * Shareef Abdur – Rasheed
Kimberly Burnham * Ann White * Keith Alan Hamilton
Katherine Wyatt * Fahredin Shehu * Hülya N. Yılmaz
Teresa E. Gallion * Jackie Allen * William S. Peters, Sr.

The Year of the Poet II
August 2015

Peridot

Featured Poets

Gayle Howell
Ann Chalasz
Christopher Schultz

The Poetry Posse 2015
Jamie Bond * Gail Weston Shazor * Albert 'Infinite' Carrasco
Siddartha Beth Pierce * Janet P. Caldwell * Tony Henninger
Joe DaVerbal Minddancer * Neetu Wali * Shareef Abdur – Rasheed
Kimberly Burnham * Ann White * Keith Alan Hamilton
Katherine Wyatt * Fahredin Shehu * Hülya N. Yılmaz
Teresa E. Gallion * Jackie Allen * William S. Peters, Sr.

Now Available

www.innerchildpress.com/the-year-of-the-poet

The Year of the Poet II
September 2015

Featured Poets
Alfreda Ghee * Lonnetce Weeks Badley * Demetrios Trifiatis

Sapphires

The Poetry Posse 2015

Jamie Bond * Gail Weston Shazor * Albert 'Infinite' Carrasco
Siddartha Beth Pierce * Janet P. Caldwell * Tony Henninger
Joe DaVerbal Minddancer * Neetu Wali * Shareef Abdur – Rasheed
Kimberly Burnham * Ann White * Keith Alan Hamilton
Katherine Wyatt * Fahredin Shehu * Hülya N. Yılmaz
Teresa E. Gallion * Jackie Allen * William S. Peters, Sr.

The Year of the Poet II
October 2015

Featured Poets
Monte Smith * Laura J. Wolfe * William Washington

Opal

The Poetry Posse 2015

Jamie Bond * Gail Weston Shazor * Albert 'Infinite' Carrasco
Siddartha Beth Pierce * Janet P. Caldwell * Tony Henninger
Joe DaVerbal Minddancer * Neetu Wali * Shareef Abdur – Rasheed
Kimberly Burnham * Ann White * Keith Alan Hamilton
Katherine Wyatt * Fahredin Shehu * Hülya N. Yılmaz
Teresa E. Gallion * Jackie Allen * William S. Peters, Sr.

The Year of the Poet II
November 2015

Featured Poets
Alan W. Jankowski
Bismay Mohanty
James Moore

Topaz

The Poetry Posse 2015

Jamie Bond * Gail Weston Shazor * Albert 'Infinite' Carrasco
Siddartha Beth Pierce * Janet P. Caldwell * Tony Henninger
Joe DaVerbal Minddancer * Neetu Wali * Shareef Abdur – Rasheed
Kimberly Burnham * Ann White * Keith Alan Hamilton
Katherine Wyatt * Fahredin Shehu * Hülya N. Yılmaz
Teresa E. Gallion * Jackie Allen * William S. Peters, Sr.

The Year of the Poet II
December 2015

Featured Poets
Kerione Bryan * Michelle Joan Barulich * Neville Hiatt

Turquoise

The Poetry Posse 2015

Jamie Bond * Gail Weston Shazor * Albert 'Infinite' Carrasco
Siddartha Beth Pierce * Janet P. Caldwell * Tony Henninger
Joe DaVerbal Minddancer * Neetu Wali * Shareef Abdur – Rasheed
Kimberly Burnham * Ann White * Keith Alan Hamilton
Katherine Wyatt * Fahredin Shehu * Hülya N. Yılmaz
Teresa E. Gallion * Jackie Allen * William S. Peters, Sr.

Now Available

www.innerchildpress.com/the-year-of-the-poet

The Year of the Poet   III
January 2016

Featured Poets
Lana Joseph * Atom Cyrus Rush * Christena Williams

Dark-eyed Junco

The Poetry Posse 2016
Gail Weston Shazor * Jron Jakubezak Vel Ratryjalskn * Jton J. White
Fahredin Shehu * Hrishikesh Padhye * Janet P. Coldwell
Joe DaVerbal Minddancer * Sharod Abdur * Rashood
Albert Carrasco * Kimberly Burnham * Keith Alan Hamilton
Hulya N. Yilmaz * Demetrios Trifiatis * Alan W. Jeskowski
Teresa E. Gallion * Jackie Davis Allen * William S. Peters, Sr.

The Year of the Poet   III
February 2016

Featured Poets
Anthony Arnold
Anna Chalasz
De Tralin El-charme

Puffin

The Poetry Posse 2016
Gail Weston Shazor * Joe DaVerbal Min... * Alfreda Ghee
Fahredin Shehu * Hrishikesh Padhye * Janet P. Coldwell
Jtone Jakubezak Vel Ratryjalskn * Sharod Abdur * Rashood
Albert Carrasco * Kimberly Burnham * Jton J. White
Hulya N. Yilmaz * Demetrios Trifiatis * Alan W. Jeskowski
Teresa E. Gallion * Jackie Davis Allen * William S. Peters, Sr.

The Year of the Poet   III
March 2016

Featured Poets
Jeton Kelmendi   Nizar Sartawi   Sami Muhanna

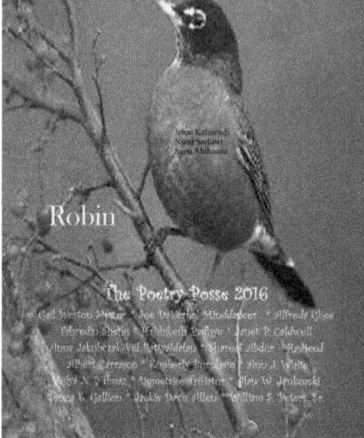

Robin

The Poetry Posse 2016
Gail Weston Shazor * Joe DaVerbal Minddancer * Alfreda Ghee
Fahredin Shehu * Hrishikesh Padhye * Janet P. Coldwell
Jtone Jakubezak Vel Ratryjalskn * Sharod Abdur * Rashood
Albert Carrasco * Kimberly Burnham * Jton J. White
Hulya N. Yilmaz * Demetrios Trifiatis * Alan W. Jeskowski
Teresa E. Gallion * Jackie Davis Allen * William S. Peters, Sr.

The Year of the Poet   III

Featured Poets

Ali Abdolrezaei

Anna Chalasz

Agim Vinca

Ceri Naz

Black Capped Chickadee

The Poetry Posse 2016
Gail Weston Shazor * Joe DaVerbal Minddancer * Alfreda Ghee
Fahredin Shehu * Hrishikesh Padhye * Janet P. Coldwell
Anna Jakubezak Vel Ratyjalslm * Sharod Abdur * Rashood
Albert Carrasco * Kimberly Burnham * Ann J. White
Hulya N. Yilmaz * Demetrios Trifiatis * Alan W. Jankowski
Teresa E. Gallion * Jackie Davis-Allen * William S. Peters, Sr.

celebrating international poetry month

Now Available
www.innerchildpress.com/the-year-of-the-poet

The Year of the Poet
May 2016

Bob Strum
Barbara Allan
D.L. Davis

Oriole

The Year of the Poet III
June 2016

Featured Poets

Qibrije Demiri- Frangu
Naime Beqiraj
Faleeha Hassan
Bedri Zyberaj

Black Necked Stilt

The Poetry Posse 2016

The Year of the Poet
July 2016

Featured Poets

Iram Fatima 'Ashi'
Langley Shazor
Jody Doty
Emilia T. Davis

Indigo Bunting

The Poetry Posse 2016

The Year of the Poet III
August 2016

Featured Poets

Anita Dash
Irena Jovanovic
Malgorzata Gouluda

Painted Bunting

The Poetry Posse 2016

Now Available

www.innerchildpress.com/the-year-of-the-poet

The Year of the Poet III
September 2016

Featured Poets

Simone Weber
Abhijit Sen
Eunice Barbara C. Novio

Long Billed Curle

The Poetry Posse 2016

The Year of the Poet III
October 2016

Featured Poets

Lana Joseph
Joe Krishnamurthy R
James Moore

Barn Owl

The Poetry Posse 2016

The Year of the Poet III
November 2016

Featured Poets

Rosemary Burns
Robin Ouzman Hislop
Lonneice Weeks-Badler

Northern Cardinal

The Poetry Posse 2016

The Year of the Poet III
December 2016

Featured Poets

Samih Masoud
Mountassir Aziz Bien
Abdulkadir Musa

Rough Legged Hawk

The Poetry Posse 2016

Now Available

www.innerchildpress.com/the-year-of-the-poet

The Year of the Poet IV
January 2017

Featured Poets
Jon Winell
Natalie Shields
JamiFatima Askir

Quaking Aspen

The Poetry Posse 2017

Gail Weston Shazor * Caroline Nazareno * Shirley Mohanty
Nizar Sartawi * Jhula Jakubczak Vel Ratty Adalan * Jen Walls
Joe DaVerbal Minddancer * Shareef Abdur - Rasheed
Albert Carrasco * Kimberly Burnham * Elizabeth Castillo
Hülya N. Yılmaz * Teloeka Hassan * Alan W. Jankowski
Teresa E. Gallion * Jackie Davis Allen * William S. Peters, Sr.

The Year of the Poet IV
February 2017

Featured Poets
Lin Ross
Souhaina Fathi
Bravee Ghani

Witch Hazel

The Poetry Posse 2017

Gail Weston Shazor * Caroline Nazareno * Shirley Mohanty
Nizar Sartawi * Jhula Jakubczak Vel Ratty Adalan * Jen Walls
Joe DaVerbal Minddancer * Shareef Abdur - Rasheed
Albert Carrasco * Kimberly Burnham * Elizabeth Castillo
Hülya N. Yılmaz * Teloeka Hassan * Alan W. Jankowski
Teresa E. Gallion * Jackie Davis Allen * William S. Peters, Sr.

The Year of the Poet IV
March 2017

Featured Poets
Tremell Stevens
Francisca Ricinski
Jamit Abu Shaih

The Eastern Redbud

The Poetry Posse 2017

Gail Weston Shazor * Caroline Nazareno * Shirley Mohanty
Teresa E. Gallion * Jhula Jakubczak Vel Ratty Adalan
Joe DaVerbal Minddancer * Shareef Abdur - Rasheed
Albert Carrasco * Kimberly Burnham * Elizabeth Castillo
Hülya N. Yılmaz * Teloeka Hassan * Jackie Davis Allen
Jen Walls * Nizar Sartawi * * William S. Peters, Sr.

The Year of the Poet IV
April 2017

Featured Poets
Dr. Rachida Rarman
Neptune Barman
Masood Khalaf

The Blossoming Cherry

The Poetry Posse 2017

Gail Weston Shazor * Caroline Nazareno * Shirley Mohanty
Teresa E. Gallion * Jhula Jakubczak Vel Ratty Adalan
Joe DaVerbal Minddancer * Shareef Abdur - Rasheed
Albert Carrasco * Kimberly Burnham * Elizabeth Castillo
Hülya N. Yılmaz * Teloeka Hassan * Jackie Davis Allen
Jen Walls * Nizar Sartawi * * William S. Peters, Sr.

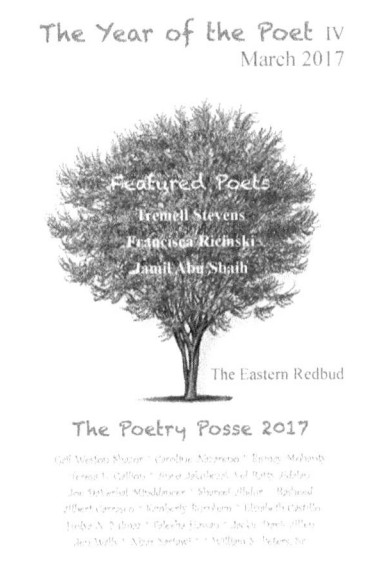

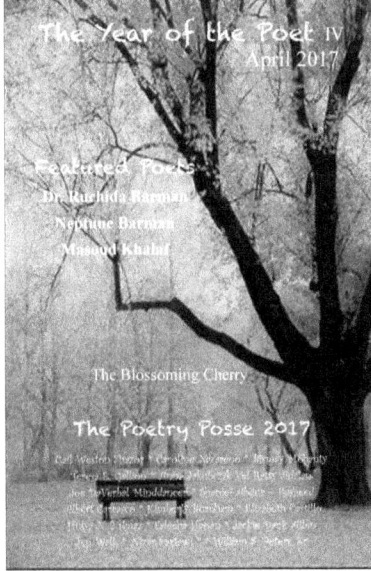

Now Available

www.innerchildpress.com/the-year-of-the-poet

The Year of the Poet IV
May 2017

The Flowering Dogwood Tree

Featured Poets
Kallisa Powell
Alicja Maria Kuberska
Fethi Sassi

The Poetry Posse 2017

Gail Weston Shazor * Caroline Nazareno * Henry Mohanty
Teresa E. Gallion * Jhana Jakubczak Val Betty Aldales
Joe DaVerbal Minddancer * Shareef Abdur – Rasheed
Albert Carrasco * Kimberly Burnham * Elizabeth Castillo
Hülya N. Yılmaz * Telosha Henson * Jackie Davis Allen
Jen Walls * Nizar Sartawi * * William S. Peters, Sr.

The Year of the Poet IV
June 2017

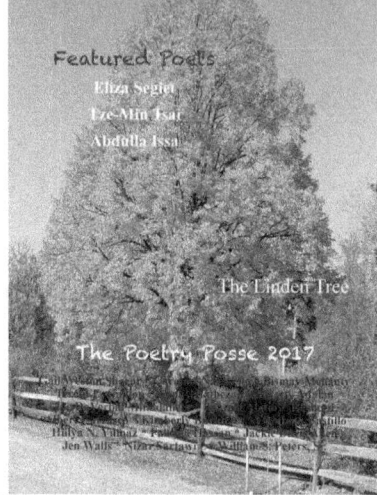

Featured Poets
Eliza Segiet
Tze-Min Tsai
Abdulla Issa

The Linden Tree

The Poetry Posse 2017

Hülya N. Yılmaz * Nizar Sartawi * William S. Peters
Jen Walls

The Year of the Poet IV
July 2017

Featured Poets
Anca Mihaela Bruma
Ibaa Ismail
Zvonko Taneski

The Oak Moon

The Poetry Posse 2017

Gail Weston Shazor * Caroline Nazareno * Henry Mohanty
Teresa E. Gallion * Jhana Jakubczak Val Betty Aldales
Joe DaVerbal Minddancer * Shareef Abdur – Rasheed
Albert Carrasco * Kimberly Burnham * Elizabeth Castillo
Hülya N. Yılmaz * Telosha Henson * Jackie Davis Allen
Jen Walls * Nizar Sartawi * * William S. Peters, Sr.

The Year of the Poet IV
August 2017

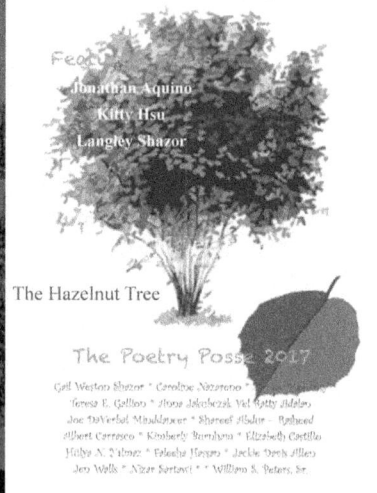

Featured Poets
Jonathan Aquino
Kitty Hsu
Langley Shazor

The Hazelnut Tree

The Poetry Posse 2017

Gail Weston Shazor * Caroline Nazareno
Teresa E. Gallion * Jhana Jakubczak Val Betty Aldales
Joe DaVerbal Minddancer * Shareef Abdur – Rasheed
Albert Carrasco * Kimberly Burnham * Elizabeth Castillo
Hülya N. Yılmaz * Telosha Henson * Jackie Davis Allen
Jen Walls * Nizar Sartawi * * William S. Peters, Sr.

Now Available

www.innerchildpress.com/the-year-of-the-poet

The Year of the Poet IV
September 2017

Featured Poets

Martina Reisz Newberry
Ameer Nassir
Christine Fulco Neal
Robert Neal

The Elm Tree

The Poetry Posse 2017

Gail Weston Shazor * Caroline Nazareno * Bismay Mohanty
Teresa E. Gallion * Anna Jakubczak Vel Ratty Adalan
Joe DaVerbal Minddancer * Shareef Abdur – Rasheed
Albert Carrasco * Kimberly Burnham * Elizabeth Castillo
Hülya N. Yılmaz * Faleeha Hassan * Jackie Davis Allen
Jen Walls * Nizar Sartawi * * William S. Peters, Sr.

The Year of the Poet IV
October 2017

Featured Poets

Ahmed Abu Saleem
Nedal Al-Qaeim
Sadeddin Shahin

The Black Walnut Tree

The Poetry Posse 2017

Gail Weston Shazor * Caroline Nazareno * Bismay Mohanty
Teresa E. Gallion * Anna Jakubczak Vel Ratty Adalan
Joe DaVerbal Minddancer * Shareef Abdur – Rasheed
Albert Carrasco * Kimberly Burnham * Elizabeth Castillo
Hülya N. Yılmaz * Faleeha Hassan * Jackie Davis Allen
Jen Walls * Nizar Sartawi * * William S. Peters, Sr.

The Year of the Poet IV
November 2017

Featured Poets

Kay Peters
Alfreda D. Ghee
Gabriella Garofalo
Rosemary Cappello

The Tree of Life

The Poetry Posse 2017

Gail Weston Shazor * Caroline Nazareno * Bismay Mohanty
Teresa E. Gallion * Anna Jakubczak Vel Ratty Adalan
Joe DaVerbal Minddancer * Shareef Abdur – Rasheed
Albert Carrasco * Kimberly Burnham * Elizabeth Castillo
Hülya N. Yılmaz * Faleeha Hassan * Jackie Davis Allen
Jen Walls * Nizar Sartawi * William S. Peters, Sr.

The Year of the Poet IV
December 2017

Featured Poets

Justice Clarke
Mariel M. Pabroa
Kiley Brown

The Fig Tree

The Poetry Posse 2017

Gail Weston Shazor * Caroline Nazareno * Bismay Mohanty
Teresa E. Gallion * Anna Jakubczak Vel Ratty Adalan
Joe DaVerbal Minddancer * Shareef Abdur – Rasheed
Albert Carrasco * Kimberly Burnham * Elizabeth Castillo
Hülya N. Yılmaz * Faleeha Hassan * Jackie Davis Allen
Jen Walls * Nizar Sartawi * William S. Peters, Sr.

Now Available

www.innerchildpress.com/the-year-of-the-poet

The Year of the Poet V
January 2018
Featured Poets
Iyad Shamasnah
Yasmeen Hamzeh
Ali Abdolrezaei

Aksum

The Poetry Posse 2018
Gail Weston Shazor * Caroline Nazareno * Tezmin Ition Tsai
Hülya N. Yılmaz * Faleeha Hassan * Jackie Davis Allen
Teresa E. Gallion * Anna Jakubczak Vel Ratty Adalan
Alicja Maria Kubenska * Shareef Abdur – Rasheed
Kimberly Burnham * Elizabeth Castillo
Nizar Sartawi * William S. Peters, Sr.

The Year of the Poet V
February 2018

Sabean

Featured Poets
Muhammad Azram
Anna Szawracka
Abhilipsa Kuanar
Aanika Aery

The Poetry Posse 2018
Gail Weston Shazor * Caroline Nazareno * Tezmin Ition Tsai
Hülya N. Yılmaz * Faleeha Hassan * Jackie Davis Allen
Teresa E. Gallion * Anna Jakubczak Vel Ratty Adalan
Alicja Maria Kubenska * Shareef Abdur – Rasheed
Kimberly Burnham * Elizabeth Castillo
Nizar Sartawi * William S. Peters, Sr.

The Year of the Poet V
March 2018

Featured Poets
Iram Fatima 'Ashi'
Cassandra Swan
Jaleel Khazaal
Shazia Zaman

Caribbean
&
Middle America

The Poetry Posse 2018
Gail Weston Shazor * Nizar Sartawi * Hülya N. Yılmaz
Jackie Davis Allen * Caroline 'Ceri' Nazareno
Alicja Maria Kubenska * Teresa E. Gallion
Faleeha Hassan * Shareef Abdur – Rasheed
Kimberly Burnham * Elizabeth Castillo
Tezmin Ition Tsai * William S. Peters, Sr.

The Year of the Poet V
April 2018
Featured Poets

The Nez Perce

The Poetry Posse 2018

Now Available

www.innerchildpress.com/the-year-of-the-poet

212

The Year of the Poet V
May 2018

Featured Poets

Zaddy Cambue de Lena X.
Sylwia K. Malinowski
Landita Ahmeti
Ofelia Pyeden

The Sumerians

The Poetry Posse 2018

Gail Weston Shazor * Nizar Sartawi * Hülya N. Yılmaz
Jackie Davis Allen * Caroline 'Ceri' Nazareno
Alicja Maria Kuberska * Teresa E. Gallion
Kimberly Burnham * Shareef Abdur – Rasheed
Faleeha Hassan * Elizabeth Castillo * Swapna Behera
Tezmin Ition Tsai * William S. Peters, Sr.

The Year of the Poet V
June 2018

Featured Poets

Brilif Maliqi * Daim Miftari * Gojko Božovic * Sofija Žrykovic

The Paleo Indians

The Poetry Posse 2018

The Year of the Poet V
July 2018

Featured Poets

Padmaja Iyengar-Paddy
Mohammad Ikbal Harb
Eliza Segiet
Tom Higgins

Oceania

The Poetry Posse 2018

The Year of the Poet V
August 2018

Featured Poets

Hussein Habasch * Mircea Dan Duta * Naida Mujkic * Swagat Das

The Lapita

The Poetry Posse 2018

Gail Weston Shazor * Nizar Sartawi * Hülya N. Yılmaz
Jackie Davis Allen * Caroline 'Ceri' Nazareno
Alicja Maria Kuberska * Teresa E. Gallion
Kimberly Burnham * Shareef Abdur – Rasheed
Ashok K. Bhargava* Elizabeth Castillo * Swapna Behera
Tezmin Ition Tsai * William S. Peters, Sr

Now Available

www.innerchildpress.com/the-year-of-the-poet

213

The Year of the Poet V
September 2018

The Aztecs & Incas

Featured Poets
Kolade Olanrewaju Freedom
Eliza Segiet
Maziee Hussain Abdul Gibair
Luis Swartz

The Poetry Posse 2018
Gail Weston Shazor * Nizar Sartawi * Hülya N. Yılmaz
Jackie Davis Allen * Caroline 'Ceri' Nazareno
Alicja Maria Kubeńska * Teresa E. Gallion
Kimberly Burnham * Shareef Abdur – Rasheed
Ashok K. Bhargava * Elizabeth Castillo * Swapna Behera
Tezmin Ition Tsai * William S. Peters, Sr.

The Year of the Poet V
October 2018

Featured Poets
Alicia Minjarez * Lonneice Weeks-Badley
Lopamudra Mishra * Abdelwahed Souayah

Bengali

The Poetry Posse 2018
Gail Weston Shazor * Nizar Sartawi * Hülya N. Yılmaz
Jackie Davis Allen * Caroline 'Ceri' Nazareno
Alicja Maria Kubeńska * Teresa E. Gallion
Kimberly Burnham * Shareef Abdur – Rasheed
Ashok K. Bhargava * Elizabeth Castillo * Swapna Behera
Tezmin Ition Tsai * William S. Peters, Sr.

The Year of the Poet V
November 2018

Featured Poets
Michelle Joan Barulich * Monsif Beroual
Krystyna Konecka * Nassira Nezzar

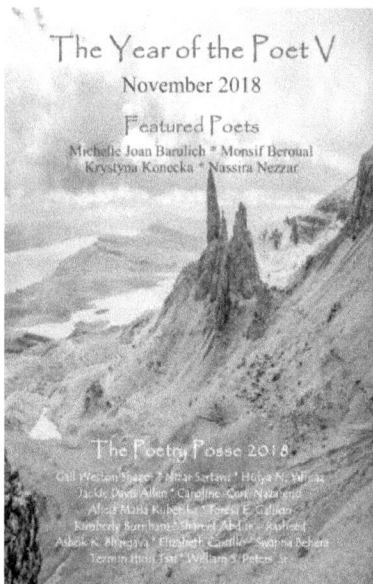

The Poetry Posse 2018
Gail Weston Shazor * Nizar Sartawi * Hülya N. Yılmaz
Jackie Davis Allen * Caroline 'Ceri' Nazareno
Alicja Maria Kubeńska * Teresa E. Gallion
Kimberly Burnham * Shareef Abdur – Rasheed
Ashok K. Bhargava * Elizabeth Castillo * Swapna Behera
Tezmin Ition Tsai * William S. Peters, Sr.

The Year of the Poet V
December 2018

Featured Poets
Rose Terranova Cirigliano
Joanna Kalinowska
Sokolović Emin
Dr. T. Ashok Chakravarthy

The Maori

The Poetry Posse 2018
Gail Weston Shazor * Nizar Sartawi * Hülya N. Yılmaz
Jackie Davis Allen * Caroline 'Ceri' Nazareno
Alicja Maria Kubeńska * Teresa E. Gallion
Kimberly Burnham * Shareef Abdur – Rasheed
Ashok K. Bhargava * Elizabeth Castillo * Swapna Behera
Tezmin Ition Tsai * William S. Peters, Sr.

Now Available
www.innerchildpress.com/the-year-of-the-poet

214

The Year of the Poet VI
January 2019

Indigenous North Americans

Featured Poets

Hpeda Elbrhtah
Anthous Brente
Ivan Eonns 'Ash'
Dr. K. K. Mathew

Dream Catcher

The Poetry Posse 2019

The Year of the Poet VI
February 2019

Featured Poets

Marek Lukaszewicz · Bhorati Nayak
Aida G. Roque · Jean-Jacques Fournier

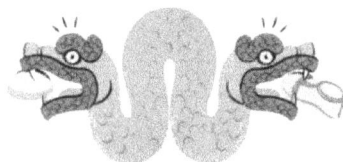

Meso-America

The Poetry Posse 2019

The Year of the Poet VI
March 2019

Enesa Mahmic * Sylwia K. Malinowska
Shurouk Hammoud * Anwer Ghani

The Caribbean

Gail Weston Shazor * Albert Carrasco * Hülya N. Yilmaz
Jackie Davis Allen * Caroline Nazareno * Eliza Segiet
Alicja Maria Kuberska * Teresa E. Gallion * Joe Paire
Kimberly Burnham * Shareef Abdur - Rasheed
Ashok K. Bhargava * Elizabeth Castillo * Swapna Behera
Tezmin Ition Tsai * William S. Peters, Sr.

The Year of the Poet VI
April 2019

Featured Poets

DL Davis * Michelle Joan Barulich
Lulëzim Haziri * Faleeha Hassan

Central & West Africa

The Poetry Posse 2019

Gail Weston Shazor * Albert Carrasco * Hülya N. Yilmaz
Jackie Davis Allen * Caroline Nazareno * Eliza Segiet
Alicja Maria Kuberska * Teresa E. Gallion * Joe Paire
Kimberly Burnham * Shareef Abdur - Rasheed
Ashok K. Bhargava * Elizabeth Castillo * Swapna Behera
Tezmin Ition Tsai * William S. Peters, Sr.

Now Available
www.innerchildpress.com/the-year-of-the-poet

The Year of the Poet VI
September 2019

Featured Poets

Elena Liliana Popescu * Gobinda Biswas
Iram Fatima 'Ashi' * Joseph S. Spence, Sr.

The Caucasus
The Poetry Posse 2019

The Year of the Poet VI
October 2019

Featured Poets

The Nile Valley
The Poetry Posse 2019

The Year of the Poet VI
November 2019

Featured Poets

Rozalia Aleksandrova * Orbinda Ginga
Sroran Ranjan Mohanty * Sofia Skleida

Northern Asia
The Poetry Posse 2019

The Year of the Poet VI
December 2019

Featured Poets

Oceania
The Poetry Posse 2019

Gail Weston Shazor * Albert Carrasco * Hülya N. Yılmaz
Jackie Davis Allen * Caroline Nazareno * Eliza Segiet
Alicja Maria Kuberska * Teresa E. Gallion * Joe Paire
Kimberly Burnham * Shareef Abdur - Rasheed
Ashok K. Bhargava * Elizabeth Castillo * Swapna Behera
Tezmin Ition Tsai * William S. Peters, Sr.

Now Available
www.innerchildpress.com/the-year-of-the-poet

The Year of the Poet VII

January 2020

Featured Poets

B S Tyagi * Ashok Chakravarthy Tholana
Andy Scott * Anwer Ghani

1901 Jean Henry Dunant and Frédéric Passy

The Year of Peace
Celebrating past Nobel Peace Prize Recipients

The Poetry Posse 2020

Gail Weston Shazor * Albert Carasco * Hülya N. Yılmaz
Jackie Davis Allen * Caroline Nazareno * Eliza Segiet
Alicja Maria Kuberska * Teresa E. Gallion * Joe Paire
Kimberly Burnham * Shareef Abdur ~ Rasheed
Ashok K. Bhargava * Elizabeth Castillo * Swapna Behera
Tezmin Ition Tsai * William S. Peters, Sr.

The Year of the Poet VII

February 2020

Featured Poets

Jennifer Ades * Martina Reisz Newberry
Ibrahim Honjo * Claudia Piccinno

Henri La Fontaine ~ 1913

The Year of Peace
Celebrating past Nobel Peace Prize Recipients

The Poetry Posse 2020

Gail Weston Shazor * Albert Carasco * Hülya N. Yılmaz
Jackie Davis Allen * Caroline Nazareno * Eliza Segiet
Alicja Maria Kuberska * Teresa E. Gallion * Joe Paire
Kimberly Burnham * Shareef Abdur ~ Rasheed
Ashok K. Bhargava * Elizabeth Castillo * Swapna Behera
Tezmin Ition Tsai * William S. Peters, Sr.

The Year of the Poet VII

March 2020

Featured Poets

Aziz Mountassir * Krishna Paraisa
Hannie Rouweler * Rozalia Aleksandrova

Aristide Briand ~ 1926 ~ Gustav Stresemann

The Year of Peace
Celebrating past Nobel Peace Prize Recipients

The Poetry Posse 2020

Gail Weston Shazor * Albert Carasco * Hülya N. Yılmaz
Jackie Davis Allen * Caroline Nazareno * Eliza Segiet
Alicja Maria Kuberska * Teresa E. Gallion * Joe Paire
Kimberly Burnham * Shareef Abdur ~ Rasheed
Ashok K. Bhargava * Elizabeth Castillo * Swapna Behera
Tezmin Ition Tsai * William S. Peters, Sr.

The Year of the Poet VII

April 2020

Featured Poets

Rohini Behera * Mircea Dan Duta
Monalisa Dash Dwibedy * NilavroNill Shoovro

Carlos Saavedra Lamas ~ 1936

The Year of Peace
Celebrating past Nobel Peace Prize Recipients

The Poetry Posse 2020

Gail Weston Shazor * Albert Carasco * Hülya N. Yılmaz
Jackie Davis Allen * Caroline Nazareno * Eliza Segiet
Alicja Maria Kuberska * Teresa E. Gallion * Joe Paire
Kimberly Burnham * Shareef Abdur ~ Rasheed
Ashok K. Bhargava * Elizabeth Castillo * Swapna Behera
Tezmin Ition Tsai * William S. Peters, Sr.

Now Available

www.innerchildpress.com/the-year-of-the-poet

The Year of the Poet VII
May 2020

Featured Poets
Alok Kumar Ray * Eden S. Trinidad
Franco Barbato * Izabela Zubko

Ralph Bunche ~ 1950

The Year of Peace
Celebrating past Nobel Peace Prize Recipients

The Poetry Posse 2020
Gail Weston Shazor * Albert Carasco * Hülya N. Yılmaz
Jackie Davis Allen * Caroline Nazareno * Eliza Segiet
Alicja Maria Kuberska * Teresa E. Gallion * Joe Paire
Kimberly Burnham * Shareef Abdur – Rasheed
Ashok K. Bhargava * Elizabeth Castillo * Swapna Behera
Tezmin Ition Tsai * William S. Peters, Sr.

The Year of the Poet VII
June 2020

Featured Poets
Eftichia Kapardeli * Metin Cengiz
Hussein Habasch * Kosh K Mathew

Albert John Lutuli ~ 1960

The Year of Peace
Celebrating past Nobel Peace Prize Recipients

The Poetry Posse 2020
Gail Weston Shazor * Albert Carasco * Hülya N. Yılmaz
Jackie Davis Allen * Caroline Nazareno * Eliza Segiet
Alicja Maria Kuberska * Teresa E. Gallion * Joe Paire
Kimberly Burnham * Shareef Abdur – Rasheed
Ashok K. Bhargava * Elizabeth Castillo * Swapna Behera
Tezmin Ition Tsai * William S. Peters, Sr.

The Year of the Poet VII
July 2020

Featured Poets
Mykola Martyniuk * Orbindu Ganga
Roula Pollard * Karn Praktisha

Norman Ernest Borlaug ~ 1970

The Year of Peace
Celebrating past Nobel Peace Prize Recipients

The Poetry Posse 2020
Gail Weston Shazor * Albert Carasco * Hülya N. Yılmaz
Jackie Davis Allen * Caroline Nazareno * Eliza Segiet
Alicja Maria Kuberska * Teresa E. Gallion * Joe Paire
Kimberly Burnham * Shareef Abdur – Rasheed
Ashok K. Bhargava * Elizabeth Castillo * Swapna Behera
Tezmin Ition Tsai * William S. Peters, Sr.

The Year of the Poet VII
August 2020

Featured Poets
Dr Pragya Suman * Chinh Nguyen
Srinivas Vasudev * Ugwu Leonard Ifeanyi, Jr.

Adolfo Pérez Esquivel ~ 1980

The Year of Peace
Celebrating past Nobel Peace Prize Recipients

The Poetry Posse 2020
Gail Weston Shazor * Albert Carasco * Hülya N. Yılmaz
Jackie Davis Allen * Caroline Nazareno * Eliza Segiet
Alicja Maria Kuberska * Teresa E. Gallion * Joe Paire
Kimberly Burnham * Shareef Abdur – Rasheed
Ashok K. Bhargava * Elizabeth Castillo * Swapna Behera
Tezmin Ition Tsai * William S. Peters, Sr.

Now Available

www.innerchildpress.com/the-year-of-the-poet

The Year of the Poet VII
September 2020

Featured Poets

Raouf Amri Al-Jishi • Srikumar Sreedaran
Dr. Brajesh Kumar Gupta • Umid Najjari

Mikhail Sergeyevich Gorbachev ~ 1990

The Year of Peace
Celebrating past Nobel Peace Prize Recipients

The Poetry Posse 2020

Gail Weston Shazor • Albert Carasco • Hülya N. Yılmaz
Jackie Davis Allen • Caroline Nazareno • Eliza Segiet
Alicja Maria Kuberska • Teresa E. Gallion • Joe Paire
Kimberly Burnham • Shareef Abdur – Rasheed
Ashok K. Bhargava • Elizabeth Castillo • Swapna Behera
Tezmin Ition Tsai • William S. Peters, Sr.

The Year of the Poet VII
October 2020

Featured Poets

Mutawaf A. Shaheed • Galina Italyanskaya
Nadeem Fraz • Avril Tanya Meallem

Kim Dae-jung ~ 2000

The Year of Peace
Celebrating past Nobel Peace Prize Recipients

The Poetry Posse 2020

Gail Weston Shazor • Albert Carasco • Hülya N. Yılmaz
Jackie Davis Allen • Caroline Nazareno • Eliza Segiet
Alicja Maria Kuberska • Teresa E. Gallion • Joe Paire
Kimberly Burnham • Shareef Abdur – Rasheed
Ashok K. Bhargava • Elizabeth Castillo • Swapna Behera
Tezmin Ition Tsai • William S. Peters, Sr.

The Year of the Poet VII
November 2020

Featured Poets

Elisa Mascia • Sue Lindenberg McClelland
Hatif Janabi • Iyau Gaëma

Liu Xiaobo ~ 2010

The Year of Peace
Celebrating past Nobel Peace Prize Recipients

The Poetry Posse 2020

Gail Weston Shazor • Albert Carasco • Hülya N. Yılmaz
Jackie Davis Allen • Caroline Nazareno • Eliza Segiet
Alicja Maria Kuberska • Teresa E. Gallion • Joe Paire
Kimberly Burnham • Shareef Abdur – Rasheed
Ashok K. Bhargava • Elizabeth Castillo • Swapna Behera
Tezmin Ition Tsai • William S. Peters, Sr.

The Year of the Poet VII
December 2020

Featured Poets

Ratan Ghosh • Ibtisam Ibrahim Al-Asady
Brindha Vinodh • Selma Kopic

Abiy Ahmed Ali ~ 2019

The Year of Peace
Celebrating past Nobel Peace Prize Recipients

The Poetry Posse 2020

Gail Weston Shazor • Albert Carasco • Hülya N. Yılmaz
Jackie Davis Allen • Caroline Nazareno • Eliza Segiet
Alicja Maria Kuberska • Teresa E. Gallion • Joe Paire
Kimberly Burnham • Shareef Abdur – Rasheed
Ashok K. Bhargava • Elizabeth Castillo • Swapna Behera
Tezmin Ition Tsai • William S. Peters, Sr.

Now Available

www.innerchildpress.com/the-year-of-the-poet

The Year of the Poet VIII
January 2021

Featured Global Poets
Andrew Scott * Debaprasanna Biswas
Shakil Kalam * Changming Yuan

Banksy's The Girl with the Pierced Eardrum

Poetry ... Ekphrasticly Speaking
The Poetry Posse 2020

Gail Weston Shazor * Albert Carasco * Hülya N. Yılmaz
Jackie Davis Allen * Caroline Nazareno * Eliza Segiet
Alicja Maria Kuberska * Teresa E. Gallion * Joe Paire
Kimberly Burnham * Shareef Abdur – Rasheed
Ashok K. Bhargava * Elizabeth Castillo * Swapna Behera
Tezmin Ition Tsai * William S. Peters, Sr.

The Year of the Poet VIII
February 2021

Featured Global Poets
T. Ramesh Babu * Ruchida Barman
Neptune Barman * Faleeha Hassan

Emory Douglas : 1968 Olympics mural

Poetry ... Ekphrasticly Speaking
The Poetry Posse 2021

Gail Weston Shazor * Albert Carasco * Hülya N. Yılmaz
Jackie Davis Allen * Caroline Nazareno * Eliza Segiet
Alicja Maria Kuberska * Teresa E. Gallion * Joe Paire
Kimberly Burnham * Shareef Abdur – Rasheed
Ashok K. Bhargava * Elizabeth Castillo * Swapna Behera
Tezmin Ition Tsai * William S. Peters, Sr.

The Year of the Poet VIII
March 2021

Featured Global Poets
Claudia Piccinto * Mohammed Jabr
Luzviminda Rivera *Nigar Arif

Tatyana Fazlalizadeh

Poetry ... Ekphrasticly Speaking
The Poetry Posse 2021

Gail Weston Shazor * Albert Carasco * Hülya N. Yılmaz
Jackie Davis Allen * Caroline Nazareno * Eliza Segiet
Alicja Maria Kuberska * Teresa E. Gallion * Joe Paire
Kimberly Burnham * Shareef Abdur – Rasheed
Ashok K. Bhargava * Elizabeth Castillo * Swapna Behera
Tezmin Ition Tsai * William S. Peters, Sr.

The Year of the Poet VIII
April 2021

Featured Global Poets
Katarzyna Brus- Sawczuk * Anwesha Paul
Rozalia Aleksandrova * Shahid Abbas

Pablo O'Higgins

Poetry ... Ekphrasticly Speaking
The Poetry Posse 2021

Gail Weston Shazor * Albert Carasco * Hülya N. Yılmaz
Jackie Davis Allen * Caroline Nazareno * Eliza Segiet
Alicja Maria Kuberska * Teresa E. Gallion * Joe Paire
Kimberly Burnham * Shareef Abdur – Rasheed
Ashok K. Bhargava * Elizabeth Castillo * Swapna Behera
Tezmin Ition Tsai * William S. Peters, Sr.

Now Available

www.innerchildpress.com/the-year-of-the-poet

The Year of the Poet VIII
May 2021

Featured Global Poets
Paramita Mukherjee Mullick * Rose Zerguine
Jaydeep Sarangi * Bismay Mohanty

Diego Rivera

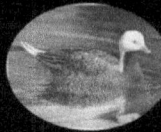

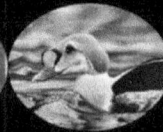

Poetry . . . Ekphrasticly Speaking
The Poetry Posse 2021

Gail Weston Shazor * Albert Carasco * Hülya N. Yılmaz
Jackie Davis Allen * Caroline Nazareno * Eliza Segiet
Alicja Maria Kuberska * Teresa E. Gallion * Joe Paire
Kimberly Burnham * Shareef Abdur – Rasheed
Ashok K. Bhargava * Elizabeth Castillo * Swapna Behera
Tezmin Ition Tsai * William S. Peters, Sr.

The Year of the Poet VIII
June 2021

Featured Global Poets
Alonzo "zO" Gross * Lali Tsipi Michaeli
Tareq al Karmy * Tirthendu Ganguly

Rayen Kang

Poetry . . . Ekphrasticly Speaking
The Poetry Posse 2021

Gail Weston Shazor * Albert Carasco * Hülya N. Yılmaz
Jackie Davis Allen * Caroline Nazareno * Eliza Segiet
Alicja Maria Kuberska * Teresa E. Gallion * Joe Paire
Kimberly Burnham * Shareef Abdur – Rasheed
Ashok K. Bhargava * Elizabeth Castillo * Swapna Behera
Tezmin Ition Tsai * William S. Peters, Sr.

The Year of the Poet VIII
July 2021

Featured Global Poets
Iram Jaan * Vesna Mundishevska-Veljanovska
Ngozi Olivia Osuoha * Lan Qyqalla

Goncalao Mabunda

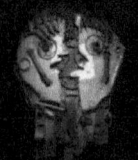

Poetry . . . Ekphrasticly Speaking
The Poetry Posse 2021

Gail Weston Shazor * Albert Carasco * Hülya N. Yılmaz
Jackie Davis Allen * Caroline Nazareno * Eliza Segiet
Alicja Maria Kuberska * Teresa E. Gallion * Joe Paire
Kimberly Burnham * Shareef Abdur – Rasheed
Ashok K. Bhargava * Elizabeth Castillo * Swapna Behera
Tezmin Ition Tsai * William S. Peters, Sr.

The Year of the Poet VIII
August 2021

Featured Global Poets
Caroline Laurent Turunc * Kamal Dhungana
Pankhuri Sinha * Paramita Mukherjee Mullick

Mundara Koorang

Poetry . . . Ekphrasticly Speaking
The Poetry Posse 2021

Gail Weston Shazor * Albert Carasco * Hülya N. Yılmaz
Jackie Davis Allen * Caroline Nazareno * Eliza Segiet
Alicja Maria Kuberska * Teresa E. Gallion * Joe Paire
Kimberly Burnham * Shareef Abdur – Rasheed
Ashok K. Bhargava * Elizabeth Castillo * Swapna Behera
Tezmin Ition Tsai * William S. Peters, Sr.

Now Available

www.innerchildpress.com/the-year-of-the-poet

The Year of the Poet IX

January 2022

Featured Global Poets

Ratan Ghosh * Christine Neil-Wright
Andrew Scott * Ashok Kumar

Climate Change : The Ice Cap

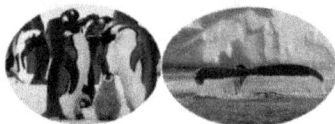

Poetry . . . Ekphrasticly Speaking

The Poetry Posse 2021

Gail Weston Shazor * Albert Carasco * Hülya N. Yılmaz
Jackie Davis Allen * Caroline Nazareno * Eliza Segiet
Alicja Maria Kuberska * Teresa E. Gallion * Joe Paire
Kimberly Burnham * Shareef Abdur – Rasheed
Ashok K. Bhargava * Elizabeth Castillo * Swapna Behera
Tezmin Ition Tsai * William S. Peters, Sr.

The Year of the Poet IX

February 2022

Featured Global Poets

Roza Boyanova * Ramón de Jesús Núñez Duval
Mammad Ismayil * Tarana Turan Rahimli

Climate Change and Mountains

Poetry . . . Ekphrasticly Speaking

The Poetry Posse 2021

Gail Weston Shazor * Albert Carasco * Hülya N. Yılmaz
Jackie Davis Allen * Caroline Nazareno * Eliza Segiet
Alicja Maria Kuberska * Teresa E. Gallion * Joe Paire
Kimberly Burnham * Shareef Abdur – Rasheed
Ashok K. Bhargava * Elizabeth Castillo * Swapna Behera
Tezmin Ition Tsai * William S. Peters, Sr.

The Year of the Poet IX

March 2022

Featured Global Poets

Dimitris P. Kraniotis * Marlene Pasini
Kennedy Ochieng * Swayam Prashant

Climate Change and Space Debris

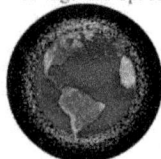

Poetry . . . Ekphrasticly Speaking

The Poetry Posse 2021

Gail Weston Shazor * Albert Carasco * Hülya N. Yılmaz
Jackie Davis Allen * Caroline Nazareno * Eliza Segiet
Alicja Maria Kuberska * Teresa E. Gallion * Joe Paire
Kimberly Burnham * Shareef Abdur – Rasheed
Ashok K. Bhargava * Elizabeth Castillo * Swapna Behera
Tezmin Ition Tsai * William S. Peters, Sr.

The Year of the Poet IX

April 2022

Featured Global Poets

Alonzo Gross * Dr. Debaprasanna Biswas
Monsif Beroual * Carol Aronoff

Climate Change and Oceans

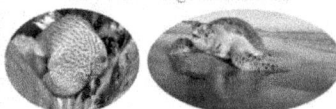

*Celebrating our 100th Edition *

Poetry . . . Ekphrasticly Speaking

The Poetry Posse 2021

Gail Weston Shazor * Albert Carasco * Hülya N. Yılmaz
Jackie Davis Allen * Caroline Nazareno * Eliza Segiet
Alicja Maria Kuberska * Teresa E. Gallion * Joe Paire
Kimberly Burnham * Shareef Abdur – Rasheed
Ashok K. Bhargava * Elizabeth Castillo * Swapna Behera
Tezmin Ition Tsai * William S. Peters, Sr.

Now Available

www.innerchildpress.com/the-year-of-the-poet

The Year of the Poet IX
May 2022

Featured Global Poets

Ndaba Sibanda * Smrutiranjan Mohanty
Ajanta Paul * Monalisa Dash Dwibedy

Climate Change and Birds

Poetry . . . Ekphrasticly Speaking

The Poetry Posse 2022

Gail Weston Shazor * Albert Carasco * Hülya N. Yılmaz
Jackie Davis Allen * Caroline Nazareno * Eliza Segiet
Alicja Maria Kuberska * Teresa E. Gallion * Joe Paire
Kimberly Burnham * Shareef Abdur – Rasheed
Ashok K. Bhargava * Elizabeth Castillo * Swapna Behera
Tezmin Ition Tsai * William S. Peters, Sr.

The Year of the Poet IX
June 2022

Featured Global Poets

Yuan Changming * Azeezat Okunlola
Tanja Ajtic * Philip Chijioke Abonyi

Climate Change and Trees

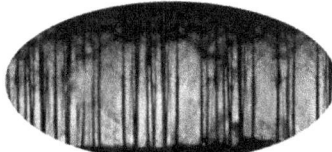

Poetry . . . Ekphrasticly Speaking

The Poetry Posse 2022

Gail Weston Shazor * Albert Carasco * Hülya N. Yılmaz
Jackie Davis Allen * Caroline Nazareno * Eliza Segiet
Alicja Maria Kuberska * Teresa E. Gallion * Joe Paire
Kimberly Burnham * Shareef Abdur – Rasheed
Ashok K. Bhargava * Elizabeth Castillo * Swapna Behera
Tezmin Ition Tsai * William S. Peters, Sr.

The Year of the Poet IX
July 2022

Featured Global Poets

Michelle Joan Barulich * Mili Das
Anna Ferriero * Ujjal Mandal

Climate Change and Animals

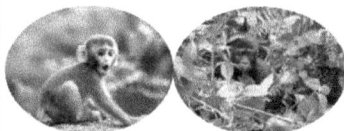

Poetry . . . Ekphrasticly Speaking

The Poetry Posse 2022

Gail Weston Shazor * Albert Carasco * Hülya N. Yılmaz
Jackie Davis Allen * Caroline Nazareno * Eliza Segiet
Alicja Maria Kuberska * Teresa E. Gallion * Joe Paire
Kimberly Burnham * Shareef Abdur – Rasheed
Ashok K. Bhargava * Elizabeth Castillo * Swapna Behera
Tezmin Ition Tsai * William S. Peters, Sr.

The Year of the Poet IX
August 2022

Featured Global Poets

Pankhuri Sinha * Abdulloh Abdumominov
Caroline Turunç * Tali Cohen Shabtai

Climate Change and Agriculture

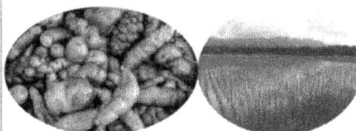

Poetry . . . Ekphrasticly Speaking

The Poetry Posse 2022

Gail Weston Shazor * Albert Carasco * Hülya N. Yılmaz
Jackie Davis Allen * Caroline Nazareno * Eliza Segiet
Alicja Maria Kuberska * Teresa E. Gallion * Joe Paire
Kimberly Burnham * Shareef Abdur – Rasheed
Ashok K. Bhargava * Elizabeth Castillo * Swapna Behera
Tezmin Ition Tsai * William S. Peters, Sr.

Now Available

www.innerchildpress.com/the-year-of-the-poet

The Year of the Poet IX
September 2022

Featured Global Poets

Ngozi Olivia Osuoha * Biswajit Mishra
Sylwia K. Malinowska * Sajid Hussein

Climate Change and Wind and Weather Patterns

Poetry ... Ekphrasticly Speaking

The Poetry Posse 2022

Gail Weston Shazor * Albert Carasco * Hülya N. Yılmaz
Jackie Davis Allen * Caroline Nazareno * Eliza Segiet
Alicja Maria Kubenska * Teresa E. Gallion * Joe Paire
Kimberly Burnham * Shareef Abdur - Rasheed
Ashok K. Bhargava * Elizabeth Castillo * Swapna Behera
Tezmin Ition Tsai * William S. Peters, Sr.

The Year of the Poet IX
October 2022

Featured Global Poets

Andrew Kouroupos * Brenda Mohammed
Carthornia Kouroupos * Faleeha Hassan

Climate Change and Oil and Power

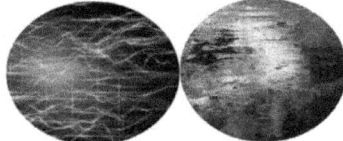

Poetry ... Ekphrasticly Speaking

The Poetry Posse 2022

Gail Weston Shazor * Albert Carasco * Hülya N. Yılmaz
Jackie Davis Allen * Caroline Nazareno * Eliza Segiet
Alicja Maria Kubenska * Teresa E. Gallion * Joe Paire
Kimberly Burnham * Shareef Abdur - Rasheed
Ashok K. Bhargava * Elizabeth Castillo * Swapna Behera
Tezmin Ition Tsai * William S. Peters, Sr.

The Year of the Poet IX
November 2022

Featured Global Poets

Hema Ravi * Shafkat Aziz Hajam
Selma Kopic * Ibrahim Honjo

Climate Change : Time to Act

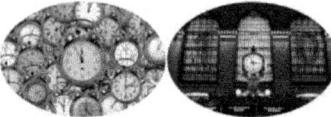

Poetry ... Ekphrasticly Speaking

The Poetry Posse 2022

Gail Weston Shazor * Albert Carasco * Hülya N. Yılmaz
Jackie Davis Allen * Caroline Nazareno * Eliza Segiet
Alicja Maria Kubenska * Teresa E. Gallion * Joe Paire
Kimberly Burnham * Shareef Abdur - Rasheed
Ashok K. Bhargava * Elizabeth Castillo * Swapna Behera
Tezmin Ition Tsai * William S. Peters, Sr.

The Year of the Poet IX
December 2022

Featured Global Poets

Elarbi Abdelfattah * Lorraine Cragg
Neha Bhandarkar * Robert Gibbons

Climate Change Bees, Butterflies and Insect Life

Poetry ... Ekphrasticly Speaking

The Poetry Posse 2022

Gail Weston Shazor * Albert Carasco * Hülya N. Yılmaz
Jackie Davis Allen * Caroline Nazareno * Eliza Segiet
Alicja Maria Kubenska * Teresa E. Gallion * Joe Paire
Kimberly Burnham * Shareef Abdur - Rasheed
Ashok K. Bhargava * Elizabeth Castillo * Swapna Behera
Tezmin Ition Tsai * William S. Peters, Sr.

Now Available

www.innerchildpress.com/the-year-of-the-poet

The Year of the Poet X

January 2023

Featured Global Poets

JuNe Barefield * Swayam Prashant
Willow Rose * Shabbirhusein K Jamnagerwalla

Children: Difference Makers

Iqbal Masih

The Poetry Posse 2023

Gail Weston Shazor * Albert Carassco * Hülya N. Yılmaz
Jackie Davis Allen * Caroline Nazareno * Kimberly Burnham
Alicja Maria Kuberska * Teresa E. Gallion * Joe Paire
Michelle Joan Barulich * Shareef Abdur – Rasheed
Ashok K. Bhargava * Elizabeth Castillo * Swapna Behera
Tezmin Ition Tsai * Eliza Segiet * William S. Peters, Sr.

Now Available

www.innerchildpress.com/the-year-of-the-poet

and there is much, much more !

visit . . .

www.innerchildpress.com/antho
logies-sales-special.php

Also check out our Authors and
all the wonderful Books
Available at :

www.innerchildpress.com/autho
rs-pages

World Healing World Peace 2020

Poets for Humanity

Now Available

www.worldhealingworldpeacepoetry.com

INNER CHILD PRESS

WORLD HEALING WORLD PEACE
2018

A Poetry Anthology for Humanity

Now Available

www.worldhealingworldpeacepoetry.com

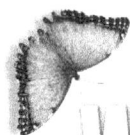

support

World Healing
World Peace

www.worldhealingworldpeacepoetry.com

World Healing World Peace
===

World Healing World Peace i am a believer !

World Healing
World Peace
2012, 2014, 2016, 2018, 2020

Now Available

www.worldhealingworldpeacepoetry.com

Inner Child Press International

'building bridges of cultural understanding'

Meet the Board of Directors

www.innerchildpress.com

Inner Child Press International

'building bridges of cultural understanding'

Meet our Cultural Ambassadors

Fahredin Shehu
Director of Cultural

Faleha Hassan
Iraq - USA

Elizabeth E. Castillo
Philippines

Antoinette Coleman
Chicago
Midwest USA

Ananda Nepali
Nepal - Tibet
Northern India

Kimberly Burnham
Pacific Northwest
USA

Alicja Kuberska
Poland
Eastern Europe

Swapna Behera
India
Southeast Asia

Kolade O. Freedom
Nigeria
West Africa

Monsif Beroual
Morocco
Northern Africa

Ashok K. Bhargava
Canada

Tzemin Ition Tsai
Republic of China
Greater China

Alicia M. Ramirez
Mexico
Central America

Christena AV Williams
Jamaica
Caribbean

Louise Hudon
Eastern Canada

Aziz Mountassir
Morocco
Northern Africa

Shareef Abdur-Rasheed
Southeastern USA

Laure Charazac
France
Western Europe

Mohammad Ikbal Harb
Lebanon
Middle East

**Mohamed Abdel
Aziz Shmeis**
Egypt
Middle East

Hilary Mainga
Kenya
Eastern Africa

Josephus R. Johnson
Liberia

www.innerchildpress.com

This Anthological Publication
is underwritten solely by

Inner Child Press International

Inner Child Press is a Publishing Company
Founded and Operated by Writers. Our
personal publishing experiences provides
us an intimate understanding of the
sometimes daunting challenges Writers,
New and Seasoned may face in the
Business of Publishing and Marketing
their Creative "Written Work".

For more Information

Inner Child Press International

www.innerchildpress.com

'building bridges of cultural understanding'

www.innerchildpress.com

202 Wiltree Court, State College, Pennsylvania 16801

~ fini ~

www.ingramcontent.com/pod-product-compliance
Lightning Source LLC
LaVergne TN
LVHW051043080426
835508LV00019B/1684